The Boss in the SHADOWS

The Life and Death of Thomas "Tommy Ryan" Eboli

Xavier Eboli
Robert Cassidy

First Edition

NEWMAN SPRINGS PUBLISHING
320 Broad Street
Red Bank, NJ 07701

First originally published by Newman
Springs Publishing 2024

ISBN 979-8-89308-991-2 (Paperback)
ISBN 979-8-89308-992-9 (Digital)

Printed in the United States of America

I am dedicating this book to my son, Michael, and my dear friend, Anthony Aversa, both of whom have been urging me to write this memoir for some time.

Introduction

Like most successful and powerful individuals, Thomas "Tommy Ryan" Eboli was a complicated man. Start first with his name. To pursue his dream of becoming a professional boxer, he assumed the name of one of his idols, the one-time welterweight champion, Tommy Ryan. The nom de guerre also helped keep his ring exploits secret from his disapproving father. While his ring career ended after his first loss, the name stuck. Early on, that proved to be a level of complexity for the numerous law enforcement agencies that tracked him. And perhaps, for some of the hoodlums with whom he consorted.

Any confusion over the name would sort itself out rather quickly.

Thomas “Tommy Ryan” Eboli spanned the American Mafia landscape like no other individual. He worked closely with Lucky Luciano, Vito Genovese, Albert Anastasia, Carlo Gambino, and Vincent “Chin” Gigante. He helped establish the foundation of the Genovese crime family and, as a member of its hierarchy, helped build it into the single most powerful criminal organization in the world. A fact that remains true to this day.

At the time of his assassination in 1972, Eboli was the street boss of the Genovese family.

Eboli was a successful businessman. Did that success follow him because he was feared, probably, but not every knuckle-dragging mobster was capable of making the moves that Thomas Eboli made. He possessed the kind of business acumen that served him well in the legitimate world. He was a boxing manager, a music executive, and the president of a vast vending machine operation that spanned New York's five boroughs. He was a man who hustled all day, but one who would never be confused with a hustler.

Inside iconic New York City venues ranging from the Copacabana to Madison Square Garden, Eboli was treated like royalty. Waiting on lines was for lesser men. Eboli was ushered in ahead of the masses or whisked through side doors, a table always ready, a pair of ringside seats always set aside. He could be diplomatic and amenable when it suited him. But when required, he could summon his temper very quickly, befitting of a man whose bookmaking operation reportedly generated $20,000 a week. He was capable of extreme generosity but, according to law enforcement, was responsible for at least twenty gangland slayings.

So powerful was Eboli that he once banned Frank Sinatra from New York City.

He was so charismatic that Tommy James, front man of Tommy James and the Shondells praised him in his book, even while Morris Levy was skimming millions of dollars from his record sales.

While Eboli would become known to many, who he really was remains unclear. Until now. The story of Thomas "Tommy Ryan" Eboli is told on these pages by his last surviving son, Xavier Eboli, a US Marine and successful businessman in his own right.

Thomas Eboli was, at turns, a proud doting father and an apathetic, absent parent. He failed to show up at Xavier's high school graduation but went to great lengths to keep Xavier from driving his car, fearing that he might be shot in a case of mistaken identity. It was a portent of things to come, as Tommy Ryan was ultimately shot and killed getting into that very car.

Not many kids are asked to endure the very public death of a parent, graphic images on the front page of newspapers or rolling across the TV screen during the evening news. But the Eboli children did. They survived and ultimately thrived. Xavier looked for answers from the men in his father's orbit, people that he knew all of his life. His questions were never really answered, but the subtle messaging was clear. Move on.

"It is important for people to know that after the trauma of our father being killed went away, we were able to carry on with our lives successfully and without the help of a guy who knew how to get things done," said Xavier Eboli.

Chapter 1

Fathers and Sons

I loved Greenwood Lake. I still do, to this day. It was an idyllic setting for a kid. At the time, I couldn't imagine a better place to grow up. It was like the entire nine-mile lake was my own swimming pool, to come and go, to swim whenever the feeling struck me. I could wander through the vast woods surrounding the lake with no fear.

I was about eight years old when, in the spring of 1948, an event took place that forever defined my relationship with my father. My mother, my two sisters, and I had walked the quarter mile from our house on Greenwood Lake to the only food store near us. When we returned home, I asked my mother if I could go swimming in the lake, and she said no. She felt that it was still too chilly and not a good day to swim.

I didn't take the answer well. Out of frustration, I threw a rock to an area of the yard where no one was standing. Now, if you've ever thrown a flat rock, you know that it will curve. At the age of eight, I had yet to realize this. So when I threw it, it curved right to where my mother was standing and hit her in the ankle.

I was so sorry and so very scared that I had hurt her. My sister Madeline and I helped her into the house and got her comfortable so she could put ice on her now-swelling ankle. The next day, which was a Friday, I knew my father would be coming up for the weekend, and I was anxious to see him. I always looked forward to him coming home from the city on weekends.

When the school bus dropped us off, I ran into the house, into our living room, and cried out, "Hi, Dad."

Well, he greeted me with a strap and gave me a beating that still stands out in my mind to this day, some seventy-six years later. He hit me relentlessly. When I fell to the floor in anguish and pain, he kicked me. He, of course, was screaming at me for throwing a rock at my mother. Through my sobs, I kept trying to explain that it was an accident.

"I didn't throw it *at* her. It curved, it curved. It was an accident."

It didn't matter. The barrage continued.

Finally, my mother had to pull him off me, saying, "That's enough, Tommy. You'll hurt him."

When he finally let me up, he sent me to the basement, and I was told to stay there until it was bedtime. I would have no dinner that night.

To make this story even worse, when he came up that weekend, he brought a good friend whom we called Aunt Millie and her son Carl.

They were witnesses to this tirade and were mortified by his abuse of an eight-year-old boy. After seeing what he was capable of, my sister Madeline feared him for many years. I also feared him and did not really care to be in the same room with him for a very long time. From that day forward, I never remember my father putting his arm around me, saying "I love you," or showing me any sign of affection.

A few years ago, I took a ride to the lake, and I drove by the log cabin that we lived in. I happened to see the current owner outside of the house. So I got out of the car, introduced myself, and told him that I lived there as a child many years ago. He was very personable, and we chatted for a while. He asked me if I'd like to see the inside. We entered the house, and outside of the modern updates to the kitchen and bathroom, it all looked very familiar. However, when we went into the living room, I froze, the memory of that awful beating became real again. It paralyzed me. I had to immediately leave that room for other parts of the house.

It remains a haunting memory of an otherwise beautiful setting. It would forever shatter the serenity of Greenwood Lake, the innocence of my childhood, and the idea that my father was my protector and my hero.

My sisters and I were completely naive when we were growing up. We had no idea who or what our father was and what exactly kept him out to all hours of the morning. We certainly wouldn't ask him where he was or what he was doing and risk having him get mad at us. His approval was something we constantly sought. In a strange way, it felt like he controlled us. He withheld his affections from us, perhaps knowing that's what we were vying for. We all sought his affection and attention. We would always look for his approval. A smile or a kind word.

Sadly, it wasn't always forthcoming.

As I got older, a picture began to develop in my head, a portrait of my father or who I believed he was. It took shape through rumor, gossip, news reports, or nuggets of a conversation he would share with me. There were certain questions I would never ask, knowing that he'd never tell me. There were things I suspected, but never confirmed. There were things I read that I didn't believe.

With the expansion of the internet and the proliferation of social media, new items have surfaced about my father over the years. Everyone seems to have an opinion on who he was and what he did. I don't pretend to have all the answers about my father. But I was along for the ride and I kept my ears open and, for the most part, my mouth shut.

One piece of new information put my father squarely in the middle of one of the most notorious Mafia shootings in history.

*****

On May 2, 1957, shortly before 11:00 p.m., Vincent "Chin" Gigante walked into the upscale Majestic Apartments on Central Park West, shouted "This is for you Frank," and fired a single bullet at Frank Costello, known in the media as the Mafia's Prime Minister.

There are mob hits and then there are mob hits that make the front page of all the newspapers. Those are generally reserved for a boss. This was one of those hits that made national news. It was about as big as it gets.

Costello was one of the architects of modern organized crime. He was a trusted associate of Charles "Lucky" Luciano, who reshaped the Mafia and turned it into a national enterprise. He did this by orchestrating the demise of Joseph Masseria and Salvatore Maranzano, two old-school bosses who ruled New York City through the 1920s. When the bloodshed was over, Luciano emerged as boss, established a national commission, and forged alliances with gangsters of other ethnicities. Vito Genovese was Lucky's underboss and Costello was his consigliere.

In 1936, Luciano was convicted of running a prostitution ring and sentenced to thirty years. In 1937, Genovese was charged with murder and fled to Italy to avoid prosecution. Costello stepped into the vacuum and became boss. Costello was dapper, clever, and cunning. You didn't survive long in that life without being able to read a few moves ahead of your competition.

Costello had become a national figure, as recognizable as Joe DiMaggio. His image played favorably in the media. There were times when the papers identified his occupation merely as "gambler," rather than what he really was, the boss. He presented himself as a businessman and acted more like a socialite than a gangster. Despite the fawning by some in the press, Costello was the most influential gangster of the 1950s. He was known simply as the Prime Minister.

While Albert Anastasia grabbed headlines for mayhem and murder, it was Costello who, for nearly two decades, was the most powerful boss in the country. He was summoned to appear before the US Senate in 1951 and testified at the Kefauver hearings. He was asked by Senator Charles Toby what he had ever done for this country as a good citizen.

"Paid my tax," said Costello.

The room erupted in laughter.

But by the late 1950s, the Mafia landscape was shifting, and Genovese had returned to the United States and wanted to consolidate power. Lucky Luciano was deported to

Italy and his influence was waning. Genovese began to make his move, and the first target was Costello. The bullet that Gigante fired at Costello in the foyer of the apartment building grazed Costello's ear and brushed against his skull. There has been much debate over the shooting of Costello. Some insist that Chin was just a bad shot and botched the job. Others argue that he missed Costello on purpose, that the ambush was a warning, and that it was time for the Chairman to step down.

Only Gigante knows for sure. Either way, it achieved the desired outcome. Frank Costello retired, and Vito Genovese took over.

*****

I was never part of that life. I never wanted it. I didn't have the temperament nor the meanness.

My father certainly didn't want it for me. Nonetheless, by virtue of birth, I was adjacent to organized crime for many years. There are those in our society who are fascinated by it and those who are turned off by it. I must admit, at times, I was both.

While researching this book, I was shown an FBI memo that identified my father as a member of the hit team tasked with taking out Costello. It was something that I had never known, and I am still not sure I believe it. FBI memos are often written on the word of confidential informants, who might have self-serving motives to cooperate. The truth is not often high on the list.

Nonetheless, I found myself familiar with all the parties involved on this historic evening.

I had known Vincent Gigante my entire life. He was a tough kid from the West Village. It has been said that in elementary school, he used to rob classmates of their lunch money.

The name "Chin" was hardly a clever underworld moniker. It came from his mother. His given name was Vincenzo; she used to call him "Chenz," which on the streets morphed into Chin. He was boyhood friends with Tony Pellone, and when he saw my father moving Tony's boxing career to the top of the welterweight division, Chin decided to turn that aggression toward the sport of boxing. He approached my father, who taught him how to box and managed his brief boxing career. My father would later mentor Vincent on his rise in the Genovese family.

I had never met Costello and heard my father speak of him only once. It was the summer of 1961, and the phone rang very late one night in our home. It woke the entire house. The next morning at breakfast, I asked my father, "Who called so late?"

"That big-nosed fuck. I told him time and time again not to call me here."

I said, "Who are you talking about?"

He said, "That fucking Frank Costello."

That was the only time I ever heard him mention his name. But by the tone of his voice, I gathered that my father had risen to a position of authority and that Costello was no longer in power.

According to the FBI memo, from 1962, it stated that my father and Fat Dom Alongi were waiting in a dark-colored sedan for Gigante outside of the apartment building. It identified my father as the getaway driver.

Dominic Alongi, also known as Fat Dom, went on to become a captain in the Genovese family, and he was very close to my father. I remember him as being physically strong and he had a reputation for being good with his hands. For a man of his size, he was extremely agile. He was about 5'6" and weighed about 275.

I played golf with Fat Dom on many occasions at the Englewood Golf Club. One time, Dom broke out laughing in the middle of the course. I looked at him, a little bit puzzled until he explained what was going on. At the time of the Costello shooting, there was a well-known model of men's underwear who seemed to show up in all the advertisements. He appeared in fashion magazines and the magazine section of the *Sunday Daily News*. The model also happened to be a friend of Frank Costello. In fact, he had dinner with Costello the night of the shooting and was at the scene when it happened. He always thought it was Fat Dom who took the shot at Costello.

"Every time this guy sees me, he takes off running," Fat Dom told me on the golf course.

Sure enough, the model happened to be playing in the next foursome, as me and Dom approached our next hole. The guy saw Dom coming, ducked out of the group, jumped in the golf cart, and took off down the fairway.

*****

In many ways, I was shielded from organized crime. While I interacted with the characters in my father's life, I was kept an arm's length from the Life.

My father, on the other hand, never had a shot.

My father, Tommaso Vito Eboli, was born on June 13, 1911, in Scisciano, a small village about thirty kilometers southeast of Naples, in Italy. My father was a large baby, and the doctor warned his mother, Maddelena, that another pregnancy could be disastrous.

My grandfather, Luigi Eboli, longed to be a gangster. It was his greatest ambition in life. My father and his parents arrived in the United States when my father was about one years old. In Chicago, Maddelena got pregnant again, but this time, she was also battling tuberculosis. The baby girl, named Rosa, died about three days after birth. Maddelena died about three months later from tuberculosis and complications caused by childbirth. As she was dying, she begged to see her son, Thomas, but they would not let my father see his dying mother out of fear that the tuberculosis could be transmitted. She cried and cried, and even though he was just two years old, my father always said he had a memory of when his mother died.

Luigi had no idea how to raise a son on his own. This could be one of the main reasons why my father had difficulty communicating and showing affection toward his own children.

Luigi had met Vito Genovese when he was a stowaway first traveling across the Atlantic. My grandfather approached Vito and desperately wanted to be part of his gang. Vito chased him, telling him he was too volatile, too unreliable, and too loud to be part of his organization. That rebuke devastated my grandfather.

When Luigi couldn't take care of my father, he left him with a sister-in-law, who only fed my father after feeding her own family. He was only given leftovers. My father would go over to the local Italian food store, owned by Saverio and Marianne Porcello, and they would feed him. Saverio was also from Scisciano. Marianne was from a nearby town called Acerra.

The Porcellos had a little girl, Mary, who would spend a lot of time with my father.

Many years later, they would marry and have three children, Madeline, Mary Ann, and Saverio, who would be me.

Luigi's greatest talent was making bathtub whiskey, which he sold to Wiseguys all over the country. On many occasions, my father would accompany him and meet these people who would later become business associates. They took notice early of Luigi's hardworking son. It speaks volumes about my grandfather that he would deny my father the opportunity to pursue a boxing career but encouraged him to become a Wiseguy.

My father was everything that Luigi was not. Quiet, efficient, and respectful. He got things done, no questions asked. As his stature rose in the Life, Luigi would become an albatross, always seeking money for a new business venture. They usually failed. Even through the 1950s, long past prohibition, he was still making homemade liquor. He once made a chartreuse that if you sampled, it would knock your socks off.

When I was leaving for the Marine Corps, my father threw a barbecue at our home. Many relatives and friends attended, and each of them left me an envelope. At the end of the party, my father asked me, "How much did Grandpa give you?"

Inside Luigi's envelope was $15.

My father shook his head. "That son of a gun. I gave him $25 to give you."

*****

It took me a long time to recover from that beating at Greenwood Lake. I slowly began to withdraw from my father. One night, he said to me, "What's wrong with you? Why are you so quiet? You used to be very happy. You'd be telling little jokes. Now, all of a sudden, you don't talk."

I told him, "My friends have fathers. I don't. We didn't have anything in common. We never did anything together. We don't go anywhere together because you are always too busy. You're too busy to do anything. My friends all talk about how they do things with their fathers. They go places, they go fishing. They go to a ball game."

My father said, "Okay, you want to go fishing? We'll go fishing."

So within a week or two, one Sunday morning, we went fishing. My mother packed up a lunch. We went out to City Island and rented a small boat. We took it out to the lower part of the Sound, and we sat there in the boat for three, maybe four hours. We sat there and didn't say a word to each other. I didn't have anything to say to him, and he didn't have anything to say to me.

There were times in my childhood where I was becoming just as indifferent as he was. When we were kids, we never asked my father what might be bothering him when he was in a bad mood. It just wasn't that kind of scenario. Even my mother knew better than to approach him when he was mad about something. Many times, we asked her, "What is it with Dad? Why is he like this?"

Her answer was usually "Well, you have to accept him for who he is, the good and the bad."

She knew what his situation was outside the home, but she would never tell us. She was never going to say, "Well, your father is a mobster." She'd never say that. Her maternal instincts helped build a layer—or a buffer—between us and the reality of our father's life.

Even after my father had passed, we'd ask her, "Did he ever tell you about that life? Did he ever tell you how they inducted him?"

She explained that she did ask him some of those questions, but my father would never talk to her about it. He was true to the code of omerta, even with my mother.

Sometimes as a kid, if you asked him a question that he didn't really want to answer, he'd say, "Can you keep a secret?"

I'd say, "Sure, of course I can keep a secret."

He'd say, smiling, "So can I."

So it wasn't all bad.

When I was twelve or thirteen years old, I used to have a newspaper route after school.

I delivered the *Bergen Record* to forty-four houses in my neighborhood. At that time, it was an afternoon paper and known as the *Bergen Evening Record*. The distributor used to drop the bundle of papers at my house around 1:00 p.m. When I got home from school, I'd fold them all up and put them into the big basket on the front of my bike. I used to go and deliver the papers Monday through Saturday.

On Saturdays, I had to collect from the customers. That paper cost thirty-three cents a week. So if they gave me thirty-five cents and told me to keep the two cents, that was going into my pocket. But I also had to pay the distributor; it was something like twenty-eight or twenty-nine cents out of the thirty-three. So if I made $5 for the total route each week, that was a lot.

On one particular Saturday, it was raining. I mean pouring rain. My father was getting dressed and getting ready to go to the city. I asked him if he could drive me around so I could collect from my customers.

He said, "Yes."

Without any barking or any complaining, my father drove me up and down, in and out of the neighborhood. We hit all forty-four houses. It probably took us two hours. When we got done, he dropped me off, I said thank you, and he said that he'd see me later.

It was a nice moment. I just wish there were more.

Many years later, I thought, if these customers only knew who was sitting out in the car waiting for me, I bet I would have gotten better tips.

I was an avid baseball player and, as a left-handed pitcher, had been pretty successful. One July 4, when I was around the same age, I was the starting pitcher for an All-Star game in Teaneck. The game was close to where we lived.

I didn't realize that my mother and father were sitting in the stands until the third inning.

That's when I first saw them. At that point, I had struck out the side the first three innings. I wound up winning the game, 8–0, and I had given up just one hit. It was the only time he came to see a game and that was because it was local and it was the Fourth of July, so he was home.

After the game, I thanked them both for coming.

My father was genuinely happy after the game, and he said to me, "You pitched a pretty good game. I didn't realize you were that good."

He never saw me play again.

*****

When I was in the eighth grade and getting ready for high school, I told my father I wanted to go to a local school in Teaneck where most of my friends were going. I also knew that it had very good athletic facilities. But my father insisted that I go to Xavier High School in New York City, which was a military, all-boys school. He said that a friend of his told him that if you want to straighten your kid out, send him there.

I didn't know I needed straightening out?

I took the entrance exam and didn't get accepted. There was a second exam, and this time, I was accepted, but I really didn't want to go. Even though I did reasonably well my freshman year, attention deficit disorder had encroached into my life, and it caused me to struggle with retention and focus. Sometime in late summer or early fall, I developed a pilonidal cyst, and I had to have an operation. It was scheduled for the middle of December, and I was in the hospital for one week. I missed the last week of school before Christmas vacation and the review of the semester. Midterm exams were held in January as soon as we got back to school. Well, I flunked three of the exams and was dismissed from the school.

My father was livid when I showed him the dismissal letter, and he insisted on seeing the school's headmaster. We went to the school, and he went into the office and met with the headmaster, and he never told me what was said. But when he came out, he said I would be allowed to take the exams again, and if I passed them, I would be reinstated.

I saw this as an opportunity to go to Teaneck High School, so I didn't pass the exams nor did I care. When we were notified that I failed, I told him, "Now, I can go to school here in town."

He said, "No. Now you can find another all-boys school and hope that they take you."

Well, I tried All Hallows in the Bronx, and they accepted me.

After I completed my sophomore year at All Hallows, I had to go to summer school. I needed to get passing grades in geometry and world history. My parents had rented a house in Long Branch at the Jersey Shore with my Uncle Pat and his family. But because of summer school, my mother insisted we only go there on weekends in order to be home for me during the week. The last week, though, they stayed down there because I had a short week with final exams. My father and I were home alone, and on the morning of the finals, I overslept.

I thought I had set the alarm properly, but I guess I didn't. Suddenly, Dad was in my room screaming at me for missing the exams. I was still sleeping. He pulled the venetian blinds off the windows and beat me while I was still in bed. When he finally stopped, I got up and ran to the bus stop to get into the city to try to take the exams. But it was too late.

I came back to the house, and he told me to take a train to Long Branch and stay there with my mother. I did as I was told, and

I stayed there until we all came home, as it was now Labor Day weekend and the rental was over. Regular school was due to start in two days after Labor Day. We came home that Monday, and I wanted to go out with my friends. Dad said I should be home by 10:30 p.m., to which I replied, "But there's no school until Wednesday. How about eleven?"

He insisted that I come home by 10:30 p.m. So I ignored him and stayed out until 11:00 p.m. When I got home and opened the front door, he came toward me with a balled-up fist. I knew that I'd better get out of there or I was going to get hit. So I jumped back off the front stoop and stood in the grass. He came out the front door and beckoned me to come inside.

I said, "You may think I'm stupid, but I'm not that stupid." And I took off running.

I stayed away for three days wandering, sleeping outside. Every now and then, I would see my mother driving my sister's car looking for me. When she finally found me at a friend's house. I agreed to come home. I told my Mom, "I'll never let him hit me again. And if he does, the next time, I'll run away, and I'll never come back."

It was, in fact, the last time he ever tried to hit me. We did not speak to or acknowledge each other after that for about three or four months.

Chapter 2

The Fight Game

It's been said that my father had a quick temper. I knew this firsthand as did many others. But in boxing and on the streets, controlling that inner rage can often be the difference between success and failure. There's a reason they call boxing the Sweet Science and for the brief time my father spent in the ring, he was able to channel his emotions into a positive fighting force.

My father started boxing when he was about fifteen or sixteen years old. He was pretty big for his age, and he was very good with his hands. He was a street fighter mostly, but he was enamored with boxing and wanted to become a professional fighter.

At that time, many of the top successful fighters were Irish. So, to be an Italian in the fight game was tough. A promoter would be far more likely to put you on his card if he though you would bring in the loyal Irish fans. So, my father adopted the name Tommy Ryan. In reality, Tommy Ryan was a welterweight and middleweight champion who fought from 1887 to 1907. My father had read that Ryan was considered the best middleweight champion in the history of the sport, up until that time. Ryan was innovative in the way he fought, boxing out a crouch. Why not borrow the name of such a legendary fighter? My grandfather, Luigi, was still determined to turn his son into a Wiseguy and he viewed boxing as a waste of time. Fighting under the name Tommy Ryan was certainly a business decision, but it also provided my father with a degree of cover from Luigi.

My father had built a 10-0 record by the time Luigi found out. He insisted that Dad retire from the ring. But my father, already showing some negotiating skills as a teenager, suggested a deal. He agreed to retire after his first defeat. It just so happened that Dad lost his next fight. He remained true to his word. Dad stepped out of the ring but didn't leave the sport.

As he got a little older, my father began managing fighters.

One of his early fighters was a promising young middleweight by the name of Salvatore "Baby" Saban. This was a tough New Yok City kid who won over fifty professional fights. Salvy was a regular at St. Nicholas Arena and even made a few appearances at the Garden. In 1938, he went ten rounds with welterweight champion Fritzie Zivic. But shortly after that bout, he got hit by a truck crossing the street and had to have his leg amputated at the hip. From that point on, my father kept him on as a trainer and to work with young fighters and help them along.

Baby Saban worked early on with both Tony Pellone and Vincent Gigante.

***

In the late 1930s and all through the 1950s, Greenwood Lake was the ideal location for a fighter's training camp. The fact that we had a home on the lake was perfect for my father and his young boxers. On the south end was Brown's Hotel, which was a training camp for many championship fighters and at the north end we had Long Pond Inn, which was also a very nice venue for fighters to train.

Most of the fighters couldn't get into too much trouble up there. It was fairly isolated.

The first contender my father managed was Tony Pellone, a real tough kid from the

West Village. Pellone was a neighborhood shoeshine boy and one day my father stopped for a shine on Thompson Street and noticed he was sporting a black eye. Pellone explained that he would often have to fight the other shoeshine boys to secure the best spot on the corner. He usually won, which meant he was making more money than the other kids.

My father asked, "Do you want to make money fighting?"

Pellone answered in the affirmative. His career began shortly after their meeting, but he also had to change his name. It was common during that era of boxing for fighters to change their names. They did it for business reasons, they did it to keep their careers a secret from disapproving family members (as my Dad did). But they also did it to enter the pro ranks at a younger age. At sixteen, Jerry Pellone was too young to become a professional fighter. But the allure of a payday and fighting at the Garden was too strong to turn down. So, he took his older brother Tony's name and went about getting a license to become a professional prizefighter at the age of sixteen and seventeen. Pellone was just seventeen years old when he hung the first career loss on welterweight contender Billy Graham, who was 52-0-6 at the time.

Tony had quite the run in 1947. He beat Graham in a rematch. He beat lightweight champ Bob Montgomery in a non-title fight. Then he beat contenders Chuck Taylor and Charley Fusari, who was 45-0. After many of those big wins, my father would be pictured in the newspaper with Pellone.

Whenever Tony was having a fight, or even Rocky Castellani, they used to come and stay at our house at Greenwood Lake. There were a few good reasons for that. One, my father would keep them out of the city, away from distraction. And two, he knew that they were getting a steak every night because my mother was cooking it for them. My mother used to cook liver and then wring the juice out of it so that they could drink it, which would give them the protein that was needed to keep their stamina up without getting the cholesterol from the solid meat. As a kid, I used to get such a kick out of watching them drink raw eggs.

So, I was about six, seven years old, eight years old. And I remember Tony living with us and even entertaining his fiancée, Lucy, who later on became his wife. Lucy was a lot of fun. She couldn't have been more than eighteen or nineteen years old. Tony was a fine addition to the house and he was very astute and religious about his training. He followed the rules that needed to be followed. He did not create or look for any distractions. And my father used to treat him more like a son. It was more than just a business relationship.

They were best friends. He was the best man at Tony's wedding. My Uncle Pat was one of the groomsmen. Rocky Castellani was another one of the groomsmen, a fellow by the name of Frankie D'Appolito was also, I believe, in the wedding party. He was another young fellow who wanted to be a fighter but didn't reach the success that Tony did. The Daily Mirror ran a photo spread of Tony's wedding. One of the featured photos was of my mother and father dancing next to Tony and Lucy.

One time, my father and Tony went out fishing on Greenwood Lake. They were enjoying a nice afternoon when a boat nearby capsized. My father steered his boat over to two men floundering in the lake and they pulled them out of the water. When the game warden got involved, my father and Tony were arrested for fishing without a license. The charges against my father were dropped, but Tony was found guilty and fined. My father filed this incident under, "No Good Deed Goes Unpunished."

A short time later, Dad began managing Castellani. Rocky also spent time with us at Greenwood Lake and he stayed at our home in Teaneck, New Jersey. I was a bit older now and I spent more time with Castellani.

When I was eleven or twelve, Rocky and I used to walk together, a mile and a half, two miles, after dinner. I would do roadwork with him in the morning. I would go to Stillman's Gym with him if I wasn't in school. Even at the age of twenty-four, he had enough youth in him to be willing to spend time with a twelve-year-old kid.

Castellani had a lot of patience with me, so much so that he would take me to the movies once in a while. One particular Saturday afternoon, he took me and my friend Carl, whom I mentioned earlier, to a matinee at the Oritani Theater in Hackensack, New Jersey.

This was in the summer of 1951, and I was about eleven years old and Carl would have been eight. There happened to be a bunch of rowdy seventeen or eighteen-year-old guys sitting a couple of rows in front of us. Rocky was up in the lobby talking to the managers, so he didn't really see the antics that these fellows were performing.

Carl and I wanted to leave our seats and go up to the candy counter in the lobby. These guys were also going to the lobby at the same time. One of them knocked me over the arm of an aisle seat. So, I went to the lobby and told Rocky what happened, and he proceeded to beat these five guys up.

The manager called the police and they arrived immediately. They wanted to know if anyone was pressing charges. The five boys did not want to press charges and after a request from the police, they apologized. Rocky, of course, wanted no publicity, not only for obvious reasons, but also because my father would get really mad at him for street fighting. He could have hurt his hands.

Carl and myself promised not to say anything about this, not only to Dad but to my mother and sisters as well.

One time, when Ezzard Charles was training for a title fight with Jersey Joe Walcott, my father took me and a friend up to South Fallsburg, New York to watch Charles train. At the time, as a kid, perspective of Charles was that this man is huge. I took a picture with him and in the photo I am trying to wrap both hands around his bicep. I couldn't do it. I don't know if it was because my hands were small, or his bicep muscle was just that big. Ezzard was very pleasant to my father and as I recall, very respectful.

But our life in boxing would change in just one night.

***

Attilio "Rocky" Castellani was a war hero who went on to become an idol of the boxing ring. A masterful boxer, Castellani was a true proponent of the sweet science. He fought with a precision and grace that belied his toughness.

At the age of ten, Rocky lost his mother Rose to illness. His father, Attilio, did not want his son to box. So, like many other fighters of that time (including his manager and stablemate Tony Pellone) Rocky began fighting under an assumed name. Rocky turned pro in Scranton in January of 1944. His pro debut ended in a draw and after ten pro fights, his record stood at four wins, two losses and four draws. But, like many professional athletes at the time, his career was interrupted by military service. Rocky was a U.S. Marine who took part in the invasion of Guam and Iwo Jima. He continued boxing in the Marines and became the middleweight champion of the U.S. Navy's Seventh Fleet and the island of Guam and all of China.

When Rocky returned from the service, he continued his pro career in and around Scranton, with mixed success. That's when he moved to New York. The change of scenery served him well. He was discovered by Tommy Ryan. His new manager brought him to Stillman's Gym where he began training with the legendary Ray Arcel. As he climbed the world rankings, Rocky beat an astonishing array of world-class fighters – Harold Green, Lenny Mancini, Walter Cartier, Tony Janiro, Ernie Durando, Gene Hairston and future Hall-of-Famer Joey Giardello. From 1949 to 1951, Rocky went 13-2-1. The only losses coming against fellow contender Charlie Fusari and another future Hall-of-Famer, Kid Gavilan. Castellani was closing in on a world title fight. But this was the Golden Age of boxing. Fighters fought. They didn't bide their time, waiting, hoping to have their number called. At this point in boxing history, there were no mandatory title defenses. While today there are four titles available in each of the seventeen weight divisions. During Rocky's time in the WBC, IBF, WBA and WBO didn't exist. In 1952, boxing consisted of just eight weight classes with one champion in each class.

So, Tommy Ryan did what he always did, he kept Rocky busy and kept the paydays coming. An offer came in for Rocky to fight a rematch with Durando. It would be the main event at Madison Square Garden and the payday would be good. To Ryan, it was a sound, calculated risk. Rocky had easily outboxed Durando in the first match, so much so that the New York Times headline after the first fight exclaimed, "Castellani Gives Masterly Exhibition in Outpointing Durando."

The rematch would take place on January 11, 1952. The second fight followed a similar form as the first one. Castellani was outboxing Durando early in the fight. Durando upset the rhythm of the contest with a knockdown, just as he did in the first fight. But Castellani recovered and continued his tactical dominance of Durando. In the seventh, Durando scored another knockdown. As Rocky got up, the referee Ray Miller pushed him back towards the ropes. Rocky never lost focus, looking Miller in the eyes the entire time. Miller, a former lightweight contender, suddenly stopped the fight.

All hell broke loose.

Tommy Ryan entered the ring and charged after Miller, throwing punches as the referee was backed into a corner. Miller was no slouch, he twice went ten rounds with the great champion Jimmy McLarnin. After Tommy got off several haymakers, corner men and officials separated the two men.

Eboli had been around too long to accept this quick stoppage. Castellani, as he had done before, rose from a knockdown and continued outboxing his opponent. But in the seventh round, he wasn't given a chance to continue. Miller stopped the fight. What Eboli knew, and most others did not, was that even though Al Weill was Madison Square Garden's matchmaker, he was also still silently managing fighters. One of those fighters was Durando. It was a conflict of interest for Weill to have an interest in both the promotion and one of the main event fighters.

Given that Rocky was rarely stopped in his career it was an unusual ending to the fight. Castellani had already beaten the count and was on his feet. It was a judgement call by Miller. Eboli believed that Weill had colluded with Miller to make sure Durando, an underdog, had won. It was, unfortunately, common in boxing at that time. The power structure of the Garden's boxing department – Jim Norris and Truman Gibson – were under the control of Frankie Carbo. Carbo was an ally of Tommy Lucchese and is believed to have been a Murder Incorporated trigger man. Carbo's influence ran so deep in boxing that the U.S. Senate launched a series of hearings on corruption in the sport. In 1961, Carbo was sentenced to twenty five years in prison for extorting welterweight champion Don Jordan.

After the fight, Tommy Ryan and his brother Pat dished out a horrific beating to Weill, who made the mistake of showing up in Castellani's dressing room. According to police, Weill never identified his attackers or pressed charges. The problem for Tommy was that there were about 10 reporters inside the dressing room.

The action was swift and immediate. The night of the fight, Bob Christenberry, the New York State Athletic Commission chairman, promised to suspend Eboli's managerial license.

In the papers the next morning, Eboli said, "If he wants my license, I will give it to him. I will hit him right in the mouth with it."

There were two hearings conducted at the athletic commission offices. One of the newspapers printed a tale-of-the-tape between Christenberry and Eboli.

One week later, Eboli was fined $3,000 and his license to manage fighters was permanently revoked.

The back page headline of the Daily News screamed, "Ban Fight Pilot of Life." On paper, Thomas "Tommy Ryan" Eboli never managed another fighter again. But most people knew better. Even the FBI knew that Eboli remained Castellani's silent manager. In 1952, Al Weill stepped down as the Garden's matchmaker to take over as manager of future heavyweight champion Rocky Marciano. It was later reported that Weill's contract called for 50-percent of Marciano's earnings, in and out of the ring. The standard boxer-manager contract was 33-percent. Marciano also believed Weill was stealing from him.

It should be noted, that in a rubber match in 1954, Castellani easily won a ten-round decision over Durando.

***

I wasn't around the fighters as much after that. I missed my interactions with Rocky. We'd still get ringside tickets to fights, but now we were coming in through the side door. We couldn't be as public about it.

It was because of Rocky that I enlisted in the Marine Corps. When it came time for me to go into the service and I was going in with a friend of mine, we were talking about the Navy, we were talking about the Air Force. But when it came down to it, we had to be Marines because Rocky was a Marine.

Rocky came to my wedding in 1962. A bunch of friends of mine were there and a couple of them were officers in the Marine Corps. He said to me, "All these guys were Marines?"

I told Rocky, "a lot of it had to do with you."

Rocky was very inspirational. He never talked about the war, never talked about being on Iwo Jima. I was really proud of him and I was very proud to be a Marine as well.

***

My father really enjoyed the sport of boxing. He loved the man-against-man competition and respect the fighters who climbed into the ring to put it all on the line. To my knowledge, he was never involved in fixed fights or strong-arming fighters. He wouldn't want to tarnish the sport in that way.

When Senator Estes Kefauver launched his investigation into boxing, a lot of names were dropped during the hearing. That's when middleweight champion Jake LaMotta admitted he had to take a dive in order to get a shot at the world title. But the name Thomas "Tommy Ryan" Eboli was never uttered once.

My father's relationship with Tony and Rocky was too important to him to sell them short. They both reached great heights in their careers. Unfortunately for both of them, they fought at the same time as Sugar Ray Robinson, who is considered by most historians to be the best pound-for-pound fighter in the history of the sport.

Tony was considered Robinson's gatekeeper in the welterweight division. Three fighters would go on to challenge Robinson for the title after they fought Pellone – Fusari, Taylor and Kid Gavilan. "I knew if they went they distance with Tony Pellone, I was in for a tough fight," Robinson once said.

Unlike Tony, Rocky Castellani would eventually get a world title fight. He challenged Carl "Bobo" Olson for the world middleweight title in 1954. Although he dropped Olson, he lost a 15-round decision to the champ. Rocky would get to fight Robinson as well. By this time, Robinson was campaigning as a middleweight and he fought Rocky in 1955. Although Rocky dropped the great Sugar Ray for a nine count in the sixth round, he was on the losing end of a split decision.

Looking back on it, my father was truly happy when he was in the fight game. In a way, boxing was a refuge for him. He found a sense of calm in the whirling atmosphere of the boxing gym. He could step away from the grinding, often cut-throat life of the street and focus on reaching a world title with his fighters. You could see it in all the photos that appeared in the newspapers. Whether he was posing with Castellani and members of the New York Giants baseball team, or posing with Pellone and the comedy team of Abbott and Costello, my father was always smiling.

I'm pretty sure he'd be smiling today as well knowing that Tony has been inducted into the New York State Boxing Hall of Fame. And that Rocky has been inducted into the New Jersey State Boxing Hall of Fame, the

Pennsylvania Boxing Hall of Fame and the Atlantic City Boxing Hall of Fame.

I believe that this is also a tribute to my father, who skillfully guided their careers in a manner that made them the successful contenders that they were.

***

But to my Dad, boxing was more than just what happened inside the ring. He truly cared for all of his fighters, even if they never reached the heights of Tony and Rocky and had their name on the Madison Square Garden marquee. He proved that with Baby Saban, providing him with hope and direction after his tragic accident.

He would do the same for Wayland Douglas. A welterweight, Douglas was a club fighter who once went eight-rounds with contender Bernard Docusen. The club-fighting circuit could be tough on a man. The purses were never great, the travel was inconvenient, and the club fighters were generally called into build the record of fighters with greater potential. It was the nature of boxing, a part of the sport that could be deemed as cruel, but it was entirely necessary. Sure, Wayland fought a couple of six-rounders at the Garden. But he also spent time in out-of-the-way locales like Troy or Utica or the Elks Auditorium in Providence.

Douglas retired in 1947 with a 26-13-3 record. He boxed a total of 213 professional rounds. My father respected that and never forgot Wayland Douglas. At his core, Wayland was a fighter just like Tony and Rocky and Baby Saban.

In the mid-1960s, Douglas reached out to my Dad and told him that he was going blind. He explained that the injury was a result of his boxing career. There are countless, heartbreaking stories of fighters who are left behind destitute and in poor health.

My Dad was not going to let that happen to Douglas. He paid for the operation that restored Wayland's vision and then he provided him with a job.

In 1972, Douglas had one of his boxing gloves bronzed and mounted on a plaque. He sent it to my Dad, who was very touched by it.

The inscription read:

> To the World's Greatest Manager
> And My Best Friend
> Tommy
>
> From Wayland Douglas, March 1972.

Chapter 3

A Contrast in Upbringing

As young men, both Thomas and Xavier Eboli were well traveled. The reasons for their travel, however, were vastly different.

Thomas Eboli was establishing contacts in organized crime throughout his teenage years. This was during prohibition, when he would often accompany his father Luigi across country when he was selling his "bathtub whiskey." The clientele were usually Wiseguys. They'd visit numerous cities,

Pittsburgh, Detroit, Chicago, Cleveland, Philadelphia, and Boston.

As a Marine, Xavier saw different parts of the world, traveling on an aircraft carrier to ports in the Caribbean and the Mediterranean. There were stops in exotic locations such as Cannes, Barcelona, Mallorca, Rome, and Piraeus. His father's travel experience amounted to riding shotgun with Luigi across backroads with cases of homemade booze in the back. Yet both journeys set each of them up for the future.

*****

Luigi did not have an easy life. He was left as an infant at an orphanage in Naples, Italy.

There was a big turnstile in which to put the baby. It was designed that way to conceal the identity of the person leaving him there. Once the baby was secured in the turnstile, the person would then ring a bell to notify someone that a baby had been left. When he was left at the orphanage, Luigi was very well dressed and came with a note that requested that his name be "Eboli." All other orphans would have the name of "Esposito," which means deposited. Luigi was soon adopted by Tommaso and Maria DeRosa. They were very well off, and young Luigi was spoiled.

At the age of thirteen, Luigi began to deliver coal, and one of his deliveries was to the Maddaloni family where he came to know their daughter Maddalena. She became his first wife and Thomas Eboli's mother.

As an adult, however, Luigi never had money and was always borrowing from family and neighbors. Unfortunately, when his first wife Maddalena died, he did not have enough money for a proper funeral and burial. Maddalena was buried in potter's field. Later, Saverio, my maternal grandfather, gave Luigi money to have Maddalena exhumed and brought to Mt. Carmel Cemetery.

Luigi then married a woman named Columbia. She helped finance Luigi's business and genuinely felt bad for young Thomas (my father), because Luigi was always traveling, and my father was left without a mother. Luigi and Columbia had two children—Madeline and Louis (he was known as Sonny). Before Luigi married Columbia, the young Thomas Eboli would bounce between relatives when Luigi was on the road, so Columbia told Luigi, "I'll marry you for the boy, not for you."

Eventually, Maddalena's mother and sister, Giovanina, came to Chicago. Luigi became smitten with Giovanina and took her and her mother out shopping, pretending to be rich. Luigi called his wife, Columbia, asking her to send money so he could travel back home to New York. Instead of returning home, he took the money and eloped with Giovanina to Massachusetts. At the time, Columbia was pregnant with Sonny. Luigi and Giovanina stayed in Revere, Massachusetts, for a while, which is where Pasquale Eboli (Uncle Pat) was born.

As odd as it sounds, my grandfather had taken up with his first wife's sister, Giovanina.

They had five children: Pasquale, (Pat Ryan), Ralph (LuLu), Johnny, Rosemary, and Nancy. Because his father married his mother's sister, Dad used to say, "I don't know if they are my brothers and sisters or cousins."

In the 1940s, Tommaso DeRosa was robbed by two men who stole his money and blinded him. His wife took care of him until she died. After that, a servant took care of him. So he eventually married the servant. When Tommaso died, he left everything to the servant girl. Luigi was in America, and when he heard that his adopted father had passed, he went back to Italy to claim the money. He tried to take it from the servant.

But the girl wrote a letter to my dad about the situation and he said that she should keep the inheritance. Needless to say, Luigi was furious. But at this point, my father had already established a reputation as an honorable man and his word stood.

*****

My father did not get much of an education. In fact, he only went as far as the third grade. This was primarily due to the fact that he didn't speak English. Also, he didn't have very much discipline in school because he didn't have much of a home life. This, of course, allowed him to learn the ways of the streets and led him to his chosen way of life.

However, he wanted his children to be educated so they would have opportunities to become successful in the legitimate world. He insisted that I attend men-only schools. He had the misguided idea that this was the way to go for a good education. He did not care at all what I wanted. Between not wanting to be at his choice of schools and contending with attention deficit disorder, I had a rough time getting an education. So after struggling through my first semester in college at Fairfield University, I decided that I didn't want to be there any longer. I quit and went home. Dad told me, "Now that you quit college, you need to go to work or join the army."

Well, the army didn't appeal to me, but the Marine Corps held my interest. So I joined the Marines with a longtime friend of mine, and we went in together. The three years that I spent in the Corps turned out to be the best education I could ever have gotten.

It was a long, hard journey, though, for my father. As a child, if he would get hungry, he'd ask his father to get him something to eat. Luigi would simply tell him, "If you're hungry, go and steal. I don't have any money." His home life was more "every man for himself," rather than a nurturing and loving environment. So that's what my father did. He went out and stole and figured out a way to survive. That was the beginning of him learning how to take care of himself. It set the wheels in motion for a lifestyle that he later came to regret.

The night that he told me that story, my father was at my house, and he had finished a couple of Scotches on the rocks. He got a little misty-eyed telling that story. He told me that he never asked for "this life," but it was pushed on him by his father. Luigi always wanted to be a gangster and, in some ways, lived vicariously through my father. It did not make for the healthiest of father-son relationships between Luigi and Dad.

My father said that if he had gotten an education instead, he probably could have been an executive with any large company of the day. He said he would have been a good one too, and I don't doubt that for a second. On the night he was telling me these stories, he seemed quite remorseful about the way his life turned out. I found that somewhat unusual, but perhaps the Scotch helped release those inner feelings.

One thing is certain about his relationship with Luigi. Those early years driving across country during prohibition would eventually pay off later for my father.

*****

My father had a ferocious temper and was used by the bosses as a bodyguard, an enforcer, and as a threat to keep others in line. These quiet qualities went a long way in this world of violence. In the 1930s, he had already developed a reputation as someone you did not want to be at odds with.

By 1935, Europe was at war with Nazi Germany, and it was only a matter of time before the US would be drawn into it. So my father tried to join the National Guard, but they wouldn't accept him because he wasn't a US citizen. However, when the US got into the fight, the army tried to draft him. He showed up at Whitehall Street at the appointed time and promptly caused a huge commotion. He felt that "if you turned me down once, why are you asking me to fight now?" They eventually did turn him down because he had an ex-wife and two sons and a current wife with a daughter and a son. He was the sole provider for two families.

During those years, 1944 to 1946, we really didn't have a home. My mother, my sister, and I used to spend six months at my grandparents' house in Chicago and six months at my father's aunt's house in Ozone Park, Queens.

Throughout his teens, my father was meeting Wiseguys and the young up-and-comers who were working with them.

Today, they would call it networking, but the young Thomas Eboli was forging alliances with the next generation of made men. These were people that he would do business with years later. Whoever he came in contact with, they were usually left impressed with the way Dad carried himself—quiet, respectful, but strong.

One of Dad's early contacts was Paul Ricca, who once saved Al Capone's life during an assassination attempt. Ricca was impressed with the young Thomas Eboli. So much so, that Ricca and his wife were best man and maid of honor at my father's first wedding. They would maintain a friendship that lasted until 1972, the year both men died.

In a full-circle moment, when I came home from the Marines, I would drive the newly constructed interstate highways (a much more pleasurable ride than Luigi and Dad took) to Chicago each December and deliver a carload of Italian delicacies to

Ricca. My cargo was hardly bathtub whiskey. Rather, I was bringing cases of fresh mozzarella, scamotz (smoked mozzarella), arugula, Italian olives—goods that were much more difficult to obtain in Chicago at the time. Christmas definitely came early in Chicago, as Paul would then share these delicacies with the guys in his outfit.

After one trip to Chicago, I stopped in Pittsburgh to see an uncle, Louis "Sonny" Eboli.

During the visit, Sonny said, "Take a ride with me, you have to meet someone."

"What's this all about?" I asked him.

"Your father wants you to meet someone."

We drove over to a social club, and my uncle introduced me to this guy. He was very pleasant. We talked for a while, and we had some coffee.

He told me to make sure, "You give your father my very best and that I was asking for him."

When we left, I asked my uncle, "Who is this guy?"

"He's the boss of the whole Midwest."

It turned out to be Sebastian "Big John" LaRocca. He ran everything between Pittsburgh and Chicago and was a boss for thirty years.

*****

My father's first wedding? Well, that was also a result of a trip to Chicago. Dad managed to impress a young lady, Anna Ariola. They spent some time together, and Anna was a lot more serious about the relationship than my father was.

However, Anna's brother Chester was a top lieutenant for Ricca. He carried considerable sway in Chicago and saw a perfect match for his sister. It wasn't exactly an arranged marriage, but the idea of bridging New York and Chicago Wiseguys through marriage was too good of a thing to pass up. So my father married Anna Ariola, and they moved to New York.

The main problem with the marriage was that Anna brought her mother, Ledizia, with her. Anna's mother was the matriarch of the family and lived with the newly married couple. In some circles, Ledizia was described as a witch, and she would do card readings. There is a story that she put some white powdery stuff in my father's coffee one morning, and he became obsessed with Anna. Who knows? But Dad did always tell me never to eat or drink anything whenever I went to Anna's house.

Dad always said he tried to make the marriage work, but his mother-in-law generally got her way in most matters. Everyone acquiesced to her demands. She felt—no, demanded—that she should be in control, laying ground rules for when my father was going to be home or what time he could go out. Well, that was never going to happen. I guess she ran out of the white powder in New York because the marriage didn't last very long.

My father was under Vito Genovese at this point of his life, and he consulted with him on his marital situation. Even though Anna gave birth to two sons—my brothers Louie and Tommy—my father could no longer live with his mother-in-law. With Vito's blessing, he sent them all back to Chicago.

*****

In his early twenties, Xavier had already been honorably discharged from the Marines and was carrying a carload of goodwill to friends in the Windy City. In contrast, at the age of twenty-two, Tommy Eboli took his first collar. His early twenties were much different than Xavier's. For a man who made a life in organized crime, his criminal record on paper was rather underwhelming. There were occasional arrests for vagrancy and disorderly conduct. Nothing that would put him on anyone's Most Wanted List.

While the FBI alleges that Thomas Eboli was part of twenty gangland homicides, he never spent more than a night in jail.

Chapter 4

Semper Fi

I very rarely saw my father get emotional. But one of those times was when I came home on my first leave from the Marines after being away for four months. I did three months of basic training at Parris Island, South Carolina, and then another month of advanced combat training at Camp Lejeune, in North Carolina. After that, I finally got two weeks leave. So, I flew home from Camp Lejeune into the old Idlewild Airport long before it became John F. Kennedy Airport. At that point, you still departed the place from a flight of stairs that they rolled out to the tarmac.

My father was waiting for me at the gate. When he saw me, I was so surprised, I saw that there were tears coming out of his eyes. He was so happy to see me.

That was one of the best moments of my life with him. It occurred immediately after one of the most strenuous times of my life.

Boot camp is a traumatic event for anyone who experiences it. The whole idea of Marine Basic Training is to completely break you down as a civilian and rebuild you as a Marine. It's during that process that you develop a whole new set of values and a whole new outlook on life. You start to develop confidence. You learn teamwork and you learn leadership. At the end of boot camp, you have learned how to get things done the way they should be done.

It's a grueling 12-week course and it seems like it's the longest 12 weeks of your life. I arrived there on June 13, 1958, and left on September 11.

My mother and my older sister, Madeline, drove down to Parris Island to see me graduate. They drove in my father's car, which was a black 1958 Cadillac Coupe de Ville. The drill instructors took notice of the car and when they saw two women get out of the car, they asked me who they were. I told them that it was my mother and sister.

Drill Instructor: "Boy, your family got money?"

Me: "We're comfortable."

I laugh now, when I think back at that moment. They had no idea who my father was. I am not sure that I did at the time either.

***

In 1958, there were 189,495 men in the United States Marines. I was proud to say that I was one of them. The Marines are the tip of the spear – the first ones in to fight. I was fully aware of the risks and responsibilities for which I had signed up. The amphibius assault as demonstrated in World War II on D-Day and Inchon, in Korea in 1950 – was still a favored strategy by the U.S. Military. The Marines were the men who launched such amphibius assaults. More than 25,000 Marines were killed during the Korean War, which ended just five years before I enlisted.

There is this idea, probably perpetuated by the Godfather movie, that Wiseguys frown upon those who enlist in the service. I never got that sense from my father. In fact, he was proud of me. My father never tried to talk me out of it. When I told him that I enlisted, he laughed, shook his head and said, "You're crazy."

But that was really the extent of his commentary on the matter of my enlistment. Apparently though, he did think about it and, at one point, was ready to offer me some type of exit strategy. About a year into my service, I was home on leave, and we had the following conversation. He asked me how things were going.

"Its rough," I said. "It's not easy."

"You know, if you want, I can get you out," he said.

"You could do that?" I responded.

"Yeah, we can do a lot of things."

I don't know if he really could do it. I never took him up on it. I told him that I signed up for three years and that I would stay the entire three years. As I have already stated, my inspiration for joining the Marines was the heroics of Rocky Castellani. I wasn't about to walk away because my father could have gotten me an easy way out.

In late December of 1958, I boarded the USS Independence, an aircraft carrier. Other than leave, I would remain on that ship until March 28, 1961. The USS Independence was part of the Forrestal-class of aircraft carriers, and it was designed in the early 1950s as a smaller vessel – an alternative to the Navy's class of supercarriers. The ship was built in Brooklyn Navy yard and was commissioned on January 10, 1959. It had four huge propellers, each one weighed 29 tons.

When I boarded the ship, it was still in Brooklyn Navy Yard. I would get liberty every other night and I would go home for dinner. I would take the subway all the way up to the George Washington Bridge and then take a bus across to our home. The Navy Yard was about 15 miles or so from the bridge.

It was nice to eat dinner with my family and sleep in my own bed. I just had to be back by 8:00 am the next morning.

Our first tour was to make a shakedown cruise in the Caribbean. A shakedown cruise occurs so the Navy can make sure everything associated with the vessel works properly – every mechanism on the ship, including the taking off and landing of planes was tested.

We stopped in Norfolk, Virginia for supplies and then it took us about seven days to reach the Caribbean. We went to Guantanamo Bay, Cuba and we arrived just four months after Castro took over. Castro's revolutionary army marched into Havana, forcing Fulgencio Battista into exile here in the United States. The region was very tense at the time, and it would become more so as Castro sought to align himself with the communist doctrine of the Soviet Union. So, there was no getting off the base once we arrived.

The base was completely fenced in, there was no leaving. It really was as they said in the movie "A Few Good Men," "I eat breakfast 300 yards from 4,000 Cubans who are trained to kill me."

Most of my time at sea, however, took place in the Mediterranean. It took us 30 days to cross the Atlantic, largely because we would stop and conduct air operations along the way. Our job was to provide a sense of security for the coastal countries. The fact that we always had planes in the air, and were carrying nuclear weapons achieved that objective. Our presence was to be viewed as a threat in the region.

On the Independence, it was out duty as Marines to make sure that anyone who was going near those nuclear weapons was qualified to be there. When the weapons were brought up to the flight deck to be attached to the jets, they were only handled by people with top secret clearance. There was always a Marine standing by to supervise and guard the weapons. For this reason, we all had top secret security clearance.

Our first stop in the Mediterranean was Rome. This was in 1960 and we were given two options – go see the Summer Olympics or go to see the Pope. I chose to see the Pope.

As we know now, Cassius Clay, won the gold medal in the light heavyweight division at those Summer Games. It's possible that I would have had a chance to see him fight if I made a different choice. He later became Muhammad Ali and ended up throwing the gold medal in the river when he came home.

When I heard that, it bothered me very much. They say the greatest honor you can have is to represent your country on the field of battle. The next best thing is to represent your country at the Olympics. While I understand what Ali was protesting, I feel that throwing the medal into the river was the wrong choice. There were other ways to get his point across. Countless young Americans strive for that gold medal to honor the red, white and blue.

Of course, years later, Ali refused induction into the U.S. Army. Again, that didn't sit well with me. My father's fighter, Rocky Castellani, was one of the top middleweights in the world. He served valiantly in World War II. So did Joe Louis, Sugar Ray Robinson and countless others. I respected Ali as a great heavyweight champion, but I never agreed with his stance during the Vietnam War.

In the Mediterranean, we spent most of our time in and out of Naples, Italy. But I also went to Palermo, Sicily, Piraeus, Greece, Nice, France, Barcelona, Spain, and the Island of Mallorca. We also stayed in each place for about three days, just enough time for every section of the ship to get a day of liberty.

***

My military operational specialty – or MOS – was a rifleman. Every Marine from the lowest private to the highest general to the commandant is a rifleman. You must qualify on a range. It's mandatory. I qualified in boot camp as a sharpshooter.

They told us right from the get-go that if you've never fired a rifle before, you stand a better chance of succeeding. All those guys who grew up hunting or shooting rifles were going to fall back on all the bad habits they developed. That experience was not going to help in the Marines.

I had never fired a rifle before. At that time, we were using the M-1, which was eight and a half pounds. It had a kick like a mule. I earned an experts badge, when I qualified two years later at Quantico, Virginia.

I also had a marksman badge for the 45-caliber handgun. Qualifying for that was very difficult. At that time, you didn't hold the pistol two hands like you do today. If you were firing right-handed, your left hand was actually in your pocket. Trying to aim a 45-caliber handgun, with one hand, shooting at 15 or 25 yards was very difficult.

This was peace time, so I never got to use any of those skills. Some Marines were briefly stationed in Beirut from July to October in 1958. Again, this was merely a military presence just to help stabilize a volatile region.

Nonetheless, my father told me he was proud of me.

Hearing that made me feel great. I was happy that he was finally giving me a rhetorical pat on the back. Only once in all the years that I was in business, did he suggest to me that I had a little bit of business sense. Of my tenure in the Marines, he was acknowledging directly to me, that I was excelling at something that I chose to do. It made me very happy.

I loved my time in the Marines and on board the Independence. It's a shame the old vessel didn't get the proper send off. The Independence saw action in Vietnam and during the Gulf War. Unfortunately, the military sold the hulk to the Japanese and they used it for target practice. It was sunk in the Pacific. They should have turned it into a museum.

***

When I got out of the Marine Corps, I wasn't sure what I wanted to do. I was now 21 and wanted to try college again. But Dad said, "Don't waste your time. I'll find a business for you."

At first, he planned to start a garbage route, but when he saw the price of a used truck, he decided not to do this. The garbage industry was under the control of Vito Genovese, and when he went to prison, Vito turned it over to my father. But Dad decided that he didn't have the time or inclination to be involved in the garbage industry. So, he turned it all over to his brother Pat, who took it over and did very well with it.

Even though the garbage business didn't work out for me, the opportunity to start my own insurance agency soon presented itself. My agency began to grow nicely with the influx of new business that was being sent my way by Dad's attorneys and friends. Then in

1967, another opportunity came my way – and that was the bagel business.

I was approached by someone in the bagel business. I was offered a position as a part owner by an existing partnership if I could provide the muscle in getting a wannabe off their back. They were having a problem and this character wouldn't leave them alone. He was intimidating them and they wanted him out of their lives. They weren't sure if he was connected. So, if I could get this done, I would get a percentage of the business.

I went to my father and explained the situation to him. He said, "Yeah, you can do this."

My father sent Fat Dom Alongi over to let this character know he had to leave these guys alone. This was accomplished easily because Fat Dom put the fear of God into him. Once the problem went away, Fat Dom then met with the principals in the bagel business and advised them in no uncertain terms that no matter what, nothing bad was to happen to me. If it did, they would be held accountable. If anything went wrong, he told them, I would walk away and they would take the heat.

It turned out that nothing ever went wrong. Our relationship lasted about seven or eight years and we became friends for life. We made a nice living together and at one point we had as many as 11 stores.

It was indicated in the press that my father was in control of the bagel business, but in fact, he wasn't.

Chapter 5

Charlie Lucky

Even though it was peace time, there was one incident overseas that I will never forget. I can't say that it felt dangerous, but some might think of it as a covert mission. I got to spend a lot of time with a man who was a close friend of my Dad and my Uncle Pat. A man who, in that Life was considered a legend.

When I was in the Marine Corps, I was stationed aboard the aircraft carrier USS Independence. At that time, many Navy ships had a detachment of marines aboard to provide internal security, act as special weapons guards and orderlies for the ship's captain and executive officer. We were going to make a cruise to the Mediterranean, where the U.S. was - and still is - constantly vigilant of our interests in that region of the world.

On my last visit home before we sailed, I mentioned to my father that Naples, Italy would be our home port while we were there. It was a six-month deployment. He told me that when I got to Naples, to go see a friend of his that had been deported in 1946. His name was Cockeyed Johnny. They called him that because he had a wandering eye. He told me that Cockeyed Johnny would take me to meet Charlie.

I asked, "Who's Charlie?"

My father made a face and looked at me, before saying, "Don't you know Charlie Lucky? Lucky Luciano."

And I said, "You know, Lucky Luciano?"

Boy was I naïve. It just shows that Dad never talked about his associates unless it was absolutely necessary.

Anyway, when I got to Naples, I went to Johnny's store. He made and sold picture frames. Johnny was so excited when I introduced myself to him. He blurted out, "Wait til Charlie meets you. He'll be happy to see you."

Johnny brought me to a nearby restaurant that he knew Charlie would be stopping at. He told the manager that I would be waiting and to let Charlie know I was there when he came in. I ordered a plate of pasta and waited. When Charlie arrived, the manager escorted him to my table. Even though Charlie didn't know me, he followed the waiter and greeted me.

When the introductions were over, he looked at what I was eating and said, "Don't eat that shit. Come on, we'll go eat some good food."

So, we went up to his apartment and we ate pasta with lentils. It was not only delicious, but it was the best version of Pasta e Lenticchie that I ever had.

Charlie asked me if I was "with" my father or my uncle. I told him no, that I was a Marine and not with my father. So, he knew not to talk about his or my father's business. But we certainly enjoyed each other's company. Luciano's apartment was beautifully decorated, and it overlooked the Bay of Naples. It had a magnificent view. I stayed in the Mediterranean for about six months, and we were in and out of Naples regularly. Each time we came into port, Charlie would meet me at Johnny's store and we would go to the race track, to the theater or just out to dinner. The theater was always a little hard for me to understand because it was all in Italian, but when Charlie Luciano wants to hang out with you, you just go with it. We spent a lot of time together and he taught me a game of solitaire that I still play today.

***

In August of 1960, Dad finally became a U.S. citizen and was issued a passport. Later that year, he made arrangements to leave New York and ring in the New Year in Naples. He stayed at the Excelsior Hotel and I got four days leave and stayed at the hotel with him. We spent a lot of time with Charlie. There were moments when he and Charlie would be discussing their business and I'd be there. If they needed privacy, they would move to another part of the apartment or lower their voices. I had nothing to offer to those conversations, but I was never told to leave. Both my father and Charlie felt comfortable with me around. We enjoyed the time we spent together and from what I observed, Charlie and my father were very cordial.

***

Luck Luciano is the architect of the modern Mafia. His vision was the product of a man who possessed the kind of intellect that allowed him to operate two steps ahead of his peers. With violence and guile, he created the structure of Organized Crime as it is known today. My father started working for Luciano at the age of 16, running booze for him during prohibition. It's been written that, by 1925, Luciano was earning more than $10-million a year through his gambling and bootlegging operations. Compelled by his success, Luciano began to think bigger. He surveyed the criminal landscape of Manhattan and believed he could rise to the top. Luciano's growing reputation made it easy to harness the ambition and power of a group of young gangsters for a takeover.

At that time, the upper echelon of the Mafia in the United States was run by "Mustache Petes." These were old-timers who began their criminal careers in Italy and brought old world values to crime in America. The rival bosses were Joe Masseria and Salvatore Maranzano. Luciano recognized that the greatest weakness of Masseria and Maranzano was greed and absolute power. Luciano promised his young partners an opportunity to share both revenue and power. It was any easy sell. In the span of five months in 1931, Luciano orchestrated the assassinations of both Masseria and Maranzano. He stepped into the power vacuum and emerged as the undisputed leader. Luciano's younger recruits read like a who's who – Frank Costello, Vito Genovese, Albert Anatasia, Joe Adonis, Joe Bonanno, Carlo Gambino, Joe Profaci, Tommy Gagliano, Tommy Lucchese and Meyer Lanksy. Luciano worked closely with Jewish and Irish mobsters. By the end of the year, Luciano would establish Organized Crime's ruling commission as well as New York's five families.

By 1946, Luciano had been deported to Italy but he would still run the American Mafia for nearly a decade. Luciano would receive information and money from a rotation of messengers who made the trip to Italy. My Uncle Pat became one of Luciano's most trusted couriers and closest friends. There is a lot of speculation about the relationship between Pat, my father and Luciano, and the pressure it may or may not have put on them. There are only a handful of sources that reference my father and my uncle's relationship with Luciano. The FBI files on both Luciano and Joseph Valachi touch on it as well as Luciano's book, "The Last Testament of Lucky Luciano."

There are some newspaper accounts, but any media reporting on the Mafia from the time my father and Uncle Pat were with Luciano would be extremely flawed. This was when the Mafia was impenetrable and Omertá – the vow of silence – was the bedrock principal of Organized Crime. Today it's been reduced to a cliché. But the majority of newspaper accounts from that time were leaked by law enforcement. There could be a variety of reasons not to trust such information – primarily because law enforcement might intentionally pass along misinformation for any number of reasons.

The government had not yet been able to turn a single major member of the Mafia. That, of course changed with Valachi in 1963. But until then, Wiseguys were certainly not talking to the media. The vision of John Gotti doing a walk-and-talk with a television reporter on Mulberry Street was completely unheard of in the 1930s, 40s and 50s.

The only ones who knew for sure what had happened were the principals themselves and they rarely spoke publicly about their affairs.

The credibility of Luciano's book has also been questioned. Upset that his one-time colleagues in Organized Crime refused to greenlight a movie project about his life, Luciano decided to write a tell-all book. He insisted that the book not be published until 10 years after his death. Much of the book reflects the tone of a bitter man. He lashed out hardest at those he felt betrayed him – primarily his one-time protégée Vito Genovese.

The book was said to be dictated to the author over the final year of Luciano's life. However, audio tapes of Luciano do not exist. Some of the discrepancies include Luciano opining about an event that occurred two years after his death and his attendance at meetings or events that occurred while he was incarcerated.

On the very first pages of the book, Luciano writes that my father had arrived in Naples in early 1961 to deliver the news that the commission had ruled he could not pursue a movie deal in Hollywood. According to the book, that set the tone of the relationship between my father and Lucky. Luciano had harsh words about my father throughout the book, primarily because he was the messenger who delivered the bad news.

Now, if the book is to be believed, it was likely that this conversation took place when I was in Naples with my father and Lucky. If that's true, then Luciano's resentment toward my father was a fabrication. Perhaps Lucky embellished the story for the book, or his ghost writer, Richard Hammer, created the tension to help the story arc.

But I know with certainly that my father and Charlie got along very well when I was with them.

In the book – as well as in FBI files – it has been suggested that Uncle Pat's relationship with Luciano was a cause of friction between my father and his brother. The premise was that my father was loyal to Vito but Pat was sentimental about his friendship with Luciano. Pat and Luciano grew very close. When Luciano needed to get a message to the States, he would write to Pat at his sister Rose Marie's address in Cresskill, New Jersey. In Italy, Luciano bred dogs, they were mini-Dobermans. One day a crate from Italy arrived at Rose Marie's house and it had a puppy inside. Luciano never said a word about it but we knew it was from him. Uncle Pat named the dog, "Lucky." The only thing I really remember about that dog was that it had a mean streak, strangers couldn't go near it.

In the book, Luciano claims that Vito was trying to take over the family and Luciano resented him for it. He claims that my father came to Naples to get his vote on whether or not Frank Costello should be allowed to retire. My father supposedly relayed the message that the rest of the commission already voted to allow Costello to retire in peace and that all Lucky had to do was rubber stamp it. I don't believe this to be true. My father didn't get his passport until 1960. Is it possible that he snuck in and out of the country? Absolutely. However, I don't believe my father would have risked getting caught and possibly denied re-entry to the United States. His entire life was here. To the best of my knowledge, my father only met with Luciano in Naples that one time. It's also possible that it was my Uncle Pat who came to solicit the vote. Pat stayed with Lucky on numerous occasions.

The idea that Costello would be allowed to retire may have been a ruse. Genovese would ultimately authorize assassination attempts on Costello and Anatasia, both of whom were still loyal to Luciano. Costello managed to survive but Anatasia did not. According to the book, Luciano explains that it was those defiant acts – both occurring in 1957 – that lead Luciano to get even with Genovese by sending him to prison. Working with Gambino, Tony Bender and a handful of others, Luciano devised a plot to bribe an imprisoned drug dealer to testify that Genovese and some of his aides – including Vincent Gigante – where involved in the heroin trade. The drug dealer, serving time in Dannemora, New York, was paid $100,000 to put Genovese squarely in the middle of a narcotics empire. The authorities commuted his sentence after he implicated Genovese and 23 others. In 1959, Genovese was sentenced to 15 years in prison. Gigante was sent away for seven years but was paroled after five. Luciano wrote that Costello kicked in $50,000 to make sure Gigante was sent to prison.

According to the book, Gambino insisted that my father be part of the set up, but Luciano refused because of his friendship with Uncle Pat.

What I can say definitively is that my father and Uncle Pat never spoke about Luciano around me. I can also say that they were extremely loyal to one another and if there was any tension over Luciano, it did not impact their relationship.

Uncle Pat was with Luciano the day he died. They were waiting at Naples International Airport to meet with movie Producer Martin Gosch. Luciano revived his thoughts about pursuing the movie again. After the meeting, Luciano suffered a massive heart attack and died. It has been reported that Pat tried to get the script from Gosch, but he refused to turn it over.

Chapter 6

Marriage and Family

My wedding was set for August 25, 1962. A few days before, Dad decided to have a dinner party with just the members of our family at the Englewood Golf Club, where he was a member. The dinner was a good way to catch up with our out-of-town relatives and talk about what everyone was doing.

It was a pretty quiet evening until dinner was over. The foyer of the club was decorated with wrought-iron furniture and had a huge floor-to-ceiling plate glass window that overlooked the swimming pool and the first-hole fairway. Well, my father picked up one of the chairs and threw it through the window, shattering it. He then picked up a golf club and started hitting golf balls off the carpet and down the fairway.

The activity drew a crowd of other members who came to see what was going on. When they realized who was hitting the golf balls, they quietly watched and gave him a round of applause, not wanting to incur his wrath. Everyone knew he had a terrible temper. I was once asked why he did that. My only real answer is, because he could. He was just trying to prove a point, that he could do anything he wanted at the club. The reason for this was because he had the owners in his pocket.

But this was not the only event that occurred during the buildup to my wedding.

*****

I first met my wife when we were both fifteen years old, and we dated off and on around three or four times over the years until we were about twenty-two. At that time, we decided there would be no more breakups. Each time we broke up, it was at the insistence of her mother. But now we were adults and her mother could no longer insist that her daughter not see me. The reason she had for her position was twofold. The first was that I was Catholic and they were very devout Methodists. The second was that I was Italian.

There were plenty of rumors about the Mafia, and this was around the time that Charlie Luciano passed away; my future father-in-law had issues with the Catholic Church because Charlie was given a funeral mass, and he received all the last rites of the church. I got him to agree to go to see the parish priest who would eventually marry us. But when he started to rant about Charlie being convicted of running a prostitution ring, I lost it. I told him in no uncertain terms that he didn't know the man. And that I did. I told my future father-in-law that I did not believe he was guilty of this crime. Furthermore, I told him that he wasn't fit to shine Charlie's shoes. That was the beginning of a very rough engagement, which culminated with Lynne's parents wanting to have a reception with no liquor because they were strict teetotalers.

I spoke to my father about it, and he said we could have the reception in our backyard—and with liquor. Well, when her father heard about this, he said he would not be giving her away or attending the wedding. So now it was two weeks before the wedding, and they were not coming. When they saw that we were not backing down, they relented.

However, it was only if we would agree to a dry reception as well as the one we had planned. So we had a dinner in a restaurant for the wedding party and immediate families only. They would not come to my parents' house for our backyard reception, mostly because they now knew that my father was a crime boss.

Over the years, my wife's parents only came in contact with my parents when there was a party for one of our children. Many years went by and I was extremely kind to them, but I never discussed my father with them. Eventually, I even got them to have a glass of wine when they came for Sunday dinner. All in all, they were good people and concerned grandparents. I couldn't have asked for better in-laws.

My father kept a very quiet position on my in-laws. He never said a word. He understood. He also respected my position, and he wasn't going to try to undermine me. My father was always very good with my wife; this issue did not come between their relationship.

My wife Lynne got along very well with my parents. My wife was a nurse, and she worked in a doctor's office in Teaneck, New

Jersey. She went to a small practice with an old-time doctor and worked there for about a year or so. When he retired, he sold his business to a young practitioner, and she worked for him for twenty years. She eventually became the office manager.

My father used to ask her all the time about his various symptoms. He saw that Lynne was a good woman, a good mother, and a good wife. My mother taught her how to cook, and once she learned, she cooked just as good as my mother.

My wife was besides herself when my father was killed. She certainly felt the loss. Her parents did not come to the wake or funeral for my father. I really didn't want them to. I told them that there would be cameras there, that the FBI would be there, and probably other law enforcement agencies. I didn't want to subject them to that. Quite honestly, we also wanted them to stay at home with the kids. The boys were small. Tommy was only eight, Michael was four, and Philip was two weeks old. My in-laws stayed at my house and took care of the kids.

*****

My wife was very active in managing my sons' hockey teams. She started with our oldest son Tommy and stayed with it through our youngest. She worked with the coaches, and she was basically a buffer between the coach and the parents. She took a very active role in being a fan and a mother and a confidant to all the hockey players. All the kids used to come to our house, and we'd have pool parties in the summer. Playing youth hockey was a big commitment. If you wanted to play serious hockey, if you wanted to continuously improve, you played about ten months out of the year.

The kids were hockey fans when they were growing up. They were all Rangers fans.

When we moved back from Arizona, they were just starting a hockey team at Ramapo High School in Franklin Lakes. My oldest son Tommy was playing in an outside league and was doing a lot of skating on his own. He made the high school team as a freshman.

All my sons played hockey in high school all four years. Tommy and Michael both played at Ramapo High School. My middle son, Michael, was a goalie in high school and for one of the travel teams. He was named 1st team All-League goaltender in his senior year and continued playing club hocket while earning his Bachelor's Degree at the University of Wyoming.

My youngest son, Philip, was the best out of the three of them. I had Philip go to St. Joseph's Regional High School in Montvale, New Jersey, which was a hockey factory. They were perennial all stars. By Philip's senior year, he was first team All-State, team MVP,

League MVP, and MVP of the Garden State Games. He had all the credentials.

Philip played in the US Hockey League in Minnesota and Iowa and then he was the captain of the Boston Junior Bruins. He earned a half scholarship to the University of Vermont, which was worth $10,000 per year, for a total of $40,000.

Philip was receiving calls from various people in the National Hockey League. Different teams were calling to find out what his interests were. He was sent to the 17-and-under national team tryouts in Colorado Springs when he was a senior. Unfortunately, he didn't make that team, but most of the players that were on that team wound up in the National Hockey League.

After graduating from Vermont, he was recruited to play in Holland, in the Holland Elite league. He was also invited to try out for a couple of different teams in the East Coast League.

However, he was not really interested in playing in the East Coast League, mostly because it was a fodder factory. They used you for bait and beat you up. So he went and played a year in Europe, and he did pretty well. In forty-two games, he had forty-eight points.

They asked him to come back for another year, but he declined. He didn't think he was going to get to the National Hockey League. They originally told him that he'd probably be drafted in the fifth or sixth round. But just before that particular draft year, the NHL opened its draft to Eastern European players: Czechoslovakians, Lithuanians, Russians. It was because of that, that he got shut out.

After one year in Europe, he decided to retire, and I brought him in to my collection business. I only had him do sales, and he's still there today, vice president of sales, and a 50 percent owner of the company.

*****

In around the year 2000, we decided to move to Florida. We found a lot in a gated golf community. So we had a house built, and we lived there for about thirteen years. After that, we decided to downsize, and at the same time, my wife came down with dementia. We moved into a condo, and we were only there for about two weeks and then she had to go into a nursing home. She never came home.

We had a good life together. I learned to get along really well with her parents. I have no regrets. If I had to do it over again, I would do it the same way.

Unfortunately, my father never got to see the boys play hockey. He really wasn't a hockey fan. He was a baseball fan only, first the New York Giants and then a Mets fan when the Giants moved to San Francisco.

Considering that he never came to my games when I was in school, I don't think he would have gone to a hockey game. The freezing cold rinks might have been another deterrent.

But who knows?

Chapter 7

Every Kind of Boss

Around 1970, Frank Sinatra held a benefit show to raise money for the Italian-American Anti- Defamation League at the Felt Forum. After the show, I made arrangements for a table at the Copacabana for about eight of us. It was me and my wife, my younger sister and her husband, and my two aunts, Rosemarie and Nancy, and their husbands. Anyway, we show up at the Copa, and the place is mobbed.

I made my way over to Carmine, who was the head maître d. I asked him if our table was ready. He said, "Well, we got an unexpected guest. Joe Colombo popped in on us, and we didn't have a reservation for him. So I gave him your table."

Of course, I was very disappointed, but we hung around until another table was made available. It was not as good of a table, but we got seated.

A couple of days later, I get a phone call from my mother that I should go downtown and meet with my father. He was having dinner at Joe's Restaurant on McDougal Street. When I showed up, he was holding court with a few friends. I remember that Rocky "Cross" Perrotta and Giuseppe "Pippy" Sabato were at the table. Rocky was an executive for Cross Siclare Paper Company on Thompson Street, and I knew Pippy as someone who was a gambler. Although many years later, Pippy became a made member of the Genovese Family.

My father says, "Sit down, do you want something to eat?"

"No," I said. "I'm going home for dinner." I asked him, "What's up?"

He looked around the table and then back at me and said, "This thing that happened at the Copa, what happened? Why did you let them give your table to somebody else?"

I said, "Well, you know, maybe if it was anybody else, I wouldn't have. But being it was Joe Colombo, I figured that was okay. I guess I assumed I was doing the right thing."

The anger in his voice was evident in his response. "No, you weren't doing the right thing. When you go to the Copacabana, they have got to treat you like they treat me. And when I go in the Copacabana, I'm a boss. I get treated like a boss. They have to treat you like they would treat me. We don't have these problems. When a guy like Joe Colombo walks into the Copacabana and there's no table, they're not supposed to give him your table. He's got to wait for a table, not you."

I said, "Well, I don't know what to tell you. I thought I was doing the right thing. Sometimes, I don't know who to be nice to."

I thought it was kind of funny, but he didn't think it was funny at all.

"Especially Joe Colombo," he said. "You don't give up a table for Joe Colombo."

My father was never shy about expressing his feelings, and it didn't matter who else was around—Rocky, Pippy, anybody. This setting gave him an opportunity to publicly amplify his dislike of Colombo.

I knew my father was a high ranking member of the Genovese family. But I never knew his official title within the family. I never asked, and if I did, he wouldn't have told me. All I had to go by were my observations and whatever small hints that I could get out of the newspapers. However, the truth is, I probably knew more than the newspaper reporters back then. No one associated with La Cosa Nostra would ever speak to a reporter back then. Their primary sources were leaks from law enforcement. Sometimes, I would see something in the paper and ask my father about it.

"It's bullshit," he would say. "Don't pay any attention to that."

Remember, at the time, the only member of the Mafia to have cooperated with the FBI was Joseph Valachi. He laid out and explained the entire structure of the Mafia to the Feds. But even in Valachi's groundbreaking testimony, falsehoods and embellishments existed. All this to say, the only ones who really knew where the members of this secret society. And back in my father's day, no one was talking.

What I did know about my father is that he talked like a boss and acted like a boss. That much I could see. He was a man who was treated with the utmost respect everywhere he went.

Today, with the advent of the internet, rumor, innuendo, and speculation are rampant online. If you do an online search, you might learn that Thomas Eboli was boss, acting boss, front boss, street boss, underboss, every kind of boss there is. I don't have a definitive answer—all I have are my observations. At this point, anyone who had firsthand knowledge of my father's position or status is dead.

The hierarchy of the Genovese family represents the largest and strongest Mafia family in the world. For nearly one hundred years, the Genovese leadership group has consisted of an elite breed of gangsters. They are the Yankees of organized crime. To this day, no one in the upper echelon of the Genovese family has cooperated with the authorities—the only one of New York's five families with that distinction. The intricate relationships and seemingly moving pieces at the top of the family were intentionally designed to deceive law enforcement. That's why, since Vito Genovese went to prison, there has been, and always will be, speculation as to who was and is the actual boss of the family. Since Vito's time as the public face of the family, it's been a long and winding road.

*****

Anthony Strollo, better known as Tony Bender, lived in Fort Lee, New Jersey, but at different times was part of a crew in East Harlem, controlled the New Jersey waterfront, and ran Greenwich Village.

FBI records described him as one of the most powerful and dangerous racketeers in the United States, noting that he was the head of a major narcotics smuggling ring.

He was also a bit of a chameleon.

Maybe it was the instinct necessary for survival in that Life, but he always managed to get close to those who were in power at the right time. During prohibition, he cemented his reputation as a bootlegger and hitman by working under Joe "the Boss" Masseria. He then defected to Salvatore Maranzano's side and became a top lieutenant. Just as Lucky Luciano was rising to power, he defected to Charlie Lucky's growing circle of young, ambitious Wiseguys. Whatever his talents were on the streets, his true gift was staying two moves ahead of the violent power struggles that shaped organized crime.

There was roughly a three-decade stretch, starting in the 1930s, where the leadership dynamic shifted between the boss Lucky Luciano, the underboss Vito Genovese, and the very influential Frank Costello. The fluctuation occurred because, at various times, Luciano and Genovese were fighting off prosecutions and deportations. In 1936, Luciano was sentenced to thirty years in prison for pandering, and that same year, Genovese fled to Italy to avoid a murder charge. In 1946, Luciano was finally deported to Italy.

In the midst of the uncertainty, Genovese wanted Bender to run the family and Luciano favored Costello. It would be Costello who would take over. But when Genovese returned, he and Bender plotted the assassination attempt on Costello, enlisting Tommy Eboli and Vincent "Chin" Gigante to carry out the mission. It has been widely reported that it was Bender who was the last person to meet with Costello before he was shot, offering crucial time and information to the hit team. Costello survived the shooting and was given the opportunity to retire.

According to an FBI memo, Bender and Eboli raised money for Chin's attorney. In that same memo, Chin was described as Bender's bodyguard and chauffeur.

With Costello retired, it was Genovese who took control of the Luciano family and named Bender the underboss. In Greenwich

Village, Bender ran the following nightclubs: Black Cat, the Hollywood, the Nineteenth Hole, and the Village Inn. Still in Italy, Luciano resented Genovese's power and the audacity of attempting a hit on Costello. Luciano still had considerable influence in America and set into motion a plot that would ensnare Genovese in a fake narcotics conspiracy. It was Bender who switched sides once more, meeting secretly with Carlo Gambino to assist in Luciano's complicated scheme to frame Vito.

On April 17, 1959, Genovese was sentenced to fifteen years in federal prison on the phony drug charges. Less than three years later, on April 8, 1962, Bender left his Fort Lee home and was never seen again. His remains have never been found. Joseph Valachi, the American Mafia's first major turncoat, testified that Genovese ordered Bender's murder from prison because he realized his underboss was part of the setup that sent him away. From prison, Genovese established a ruling panel to oversee the family; it consisted of Thomas Eboli, Jerry Catena, and Phil Lombardo.

*****

I met Tony Bender many times. He was a little skinny guy and not the least bit intimidating. But he probably had a big pair of balls because he was very successful on the streets. He had a big reputation that dated all the way back to the 1930s.

In the early 1950s, I was going to Xavier High School down on Sixteenth Street. Sometimes, after school, I would go down to Thompson Street and see if my father was around so I could catch a ride home. On many of those occasions, I would meet Tony. He was always there, in the same spot, at the Cafe Napoli di Notte on Thompson Street, just north of Houston Street. Tony was always in my father's life; they traveled in the same small circle of men who populated the administration of the Genovese family.

A decade later, he was gone. When he disappeared, I asked my father about it. His answer was typically vague.

"God only knows where this guy is. He's on the run. There is a rumor that he might have been fooling around with drugs. And if that was the case, he better leave town before somebody got to him."

A couple of months later, Dad told me that he was now in charge of all the night-clubs and fag joints that Tony Bender previously ran. He said that he told Matty "The Horse" Iannello that he knew he was skimming money from all these joints and that he had one week to bring him a shoebox full of money or he was going to have to answer for what he had been doing. He delivered the money.

This led me to believe that Dad had moved up the ladder to a new position, and the more I thought about it, he might have had something to do with Bender's disappearance. Of course, he would never tell me that. But around the same time, he told me that he was now the Number 2 man in the Copacabana and that "Benny Squint" was Number 1. Benny Squint's real name was Phil Lombardo, part of that ruling panel with Dad.

I just left it at that. There was nothing more to say or ask.

I ran into Tony Bender's son once in Teaneck. It was around 1964. I really didn't know what to say. He asked me if I knew anything. I wasn't sure what my dad knew about his dad or whether I should feel bad about what happened. On a human level, of course, I felt bad for him. But I didn't say much. I just said to him, "This is the life that they chose, and whatever happens, happens."

Honestly, I was glad that it wasn't my father. I know that sounds selfish, but it's true.

That's really how I felt. You start to think a little selfishly because in that Life, you never knew what could happen.

*****

Philip Lombardo a.k.a. Benny Squint had one of the lowest profiles of any boss in organized crime. He had a cross eye and wore thick glasses. Not exactly the Dapper Don the newspapers would have you believe fits the description of all mob bosses. He was only about five foot, six inches, but his reputation loomed large in the Genovese family. He started as a soldier under Trigger Mike Coppola in the notorious East Harlem crew on 116th Street and would eventually become boss of the family.

When Trigger Mike passed, Benny Squint became capo of the crew. When Benny Squint moved into a leadership role when Vito was sent to prison, Fat Tony Salerno was elevated to capo in East Harlem. Lombardo rarely made headlines and, despite being arrested on more than a dozen occasions, barely spent time in prison. It's been reported that at that time, even members of his own family didn't know he was the boss.

*****

I met Benny Squint many times. Soon after my father had a house built in Englewood Cliffs, he wanted to go to an appliance store somewhere in Harlem to buy some things that he needed for the house. This was in May or June of 1961. He was looking for a television, a couple of smaller televisions for other rooms, and a refrigerator. Benny took us all to this one appliance store. My mother and father walked around and picked out all the things that they wanted. When my father went to pay for all of this stuff, Benny told him, "No, it's all on me, I got it."

When I saw that, I said to myself, "You know, there must be something to this." I never even heard of him before we moved to Englewood Cliffs. Now, all of a sudden, he's displaying a little bit of power in a public way. This was not the move of a man trying to ingratiate himself with my dad, because I had seen that many times. This was a man who acted like paying was a nuisance for anyone in his circle. That was the first time I met him. After that, he used to come to the house regularly, and he would sit outside in the backyard with my father and talk. The conversations were always private and just between the two of them.

Then over the course of the next few years at the Englewood Golf Club, Benny used to come, and he and my father would have meetings there. They would huddle in a corner, and again, they were not to be disturbed. A couple of times, I walked over to say hello and chat, but my father told me to go away, which indicated to me that these were conversations that I should not hear.

When my father had a heart attack in 1968, Benny came to the hospital every day. My father was in Holy Name Hospital in Teaneck for one month, and Benny used to stop in and visit daily. One particular time, I was having some sort of a problem. I don't remember what the problem was, but Benny pulled me outside the room in the hallway, and he started telling me what I should do to take care of this problem.

"You do this and the problem goes away," I remember him saying.

He was sympathetic to my problem, but he was also telling me very forcefully how to resolve it. He was giving me some fatherly advice, where my own father would not give me advice like that.

But after 1968, I didn't see him that often. Occasionally, if I happened to be at my parents' apartment in Fort Lee on a Tuesday night, I'd run into him. Every Tuesday night, it turned out, Benny came to my father's apartment for a weekly update.

You can tell when somebody is a boss. This was a guy that my father showed respect to, so I thought that he must be some sort of boss. I didn't realize that he was *the* boss. It kind of bothered me to see my father being solicitous of somebody else like that because, you know, he didn't take a backseat to too many people. When Benny was around, he seemed to defer to Benny's authority. That was unusual for me to see. But that's how you figure things out. I know if I had asked, I was going to be told to mind my own business.

*****

It was Vito Genovese who came up with the concept of the "front boss." Although I do not know this for certain, what I have read and what I have seen, this scenario makes the most sense. Of the original ruling panel of Dad, Benny Squint, and Catena, Benny would emerge as the acting boss while Vito was in prison. He officially took over as boss in 1969 when Vito died. In that nine-year stretch that Vito was in prison, my father filled many roles—underboss, street boss, and yes, front boss for Benny Squint. After my father's assassination, Funzi Tieri would become front boss for Benny. When Benny retired in 1981, he named Gigante as his successor, and Fat Tony Salerno became the front boss when Funzi died in 1982. The deception was so strong that it was Salerno, and not Chin, who was sentenced to one hundred years in prison during the Commission Case.

The circles are very small and tight inside that Life. For that reason, we got to know many of the children of my father's associates. One of my sisters was friendly with one of Benny Squint's daughters. Within the last year, my sister told me that she got a call from

Benny Squint's daughter over the holidays. All these years later, that didn't sit right with me. There was no way that anyone could have killed my father without Benny's approval. As boss of the family, he had to know about it, and he had to okay it. That hurts to this day.

Chapter 8

The Music Industry

When you are "with" someone in the Mafia, the word "with" takes on a very different meaning. If someone on the street were to tell you, "I'm with Vito Genovese." That's a very powerful statement. If you are with a made guy, you are protected from a lot of things. There is of course a flip side to that. You have to pay for that privilege, and the splits are rarely in the favor of the civilian.

There were many individuals who were "with" my father. These were largely transactional relationships. Some people just represented another envelope to be picked up at the end of the week. Bert Berns was different; he wasn't just an envelope.

I honestly have no idea how my father and Bert met, but I do know how they became friends. It was an interest in boating, and they each had boats at the Edgewater Marina. They would go out on the water together, one day on his boat, one day on my father's boat. It was said in the critically acclaimed documentary about Bert Berns that they actually met at the marina. I think that's unlikely because my father would never strike up a conversation with a stranger. In my opinion, he and Bert crossed paths in some other setting, and that's when the friendship was born. Bert and my father became partners in a recording studio called Incredible Sounds. I handled the insurance for the company.

When Bert sold his boat, he gave me a shotgun and a rifle that he kept on his boat.

He told everyone the firearms were for protection, but in reality, they were there to shoot the seagulls that would fly around the boat.

Bert Berns was a songwriting legend out of the Bronx. He contracted rheumatic fever as a child, and it impacted his health for his entire life. It was a factor in his tragic death from heart failure at the age of thirty-eight. But Berns had an incredible impact in the music industry, writing hit songs that included "Twist and Shout," "Piece of My Heart," "Here Comes the Night," and "Hang on Sloopy." He also produced such hits as "Brown-Eyed Girl" and "Under the Boardwalk."

Berns rose to prominence writing and producing for Atlantic Records. In 1965, Berns left Atlantic Records and started his own label, Bang Records, with the support of Atlantic's ownership. Bert continued to churn out hit after hit and then simultaneously launched another label, Shout Records, which produced rhythm and blues and soul music.

To my father, Bert was like the fighters he had managed in the 1950s. There was a real relationship between them. My father was literally and figuratively in their corner. It was the same with Bert. There was no question that he and Bert were good friends.

When Atlantic's Jerry Wexler tried to move in on Bang Records, Bert resisted. After that, Wexler enlisted Morris Levy to put some pressure on Berns. That's when my father stepped in.

My father was partners with Levy in other ventures, but Morris had no business with Bert Berns. My father didn't care what another man did for a living, as long as it didn't affect him or anyone close to him. As long as you stayed on your side of the line, he didn't care. But if you crossed that line, he made sure you stepped back over to your side of the line. That's what happened here—Wexler and Levy left Bert alone.

When Bert died at his New York City apartment of heart failure in 1967, my father was the first one to arrive at his home. That's how highly my father thought of Bert Burns.

*****

Morris Levy was a man driven to succeed any way he could. He was a tough businessman and a very tough individual. Levy became a millionaire the first time and then lost it all by the time he was twenty-one. Along the way, he met and made money with Wiseguys all over New York. But he once told me that he would never put a Wiseguy on the payroll.

Levy started Roulette Records and all of its affiliate labels when rock and roll was still in its infancy. At that time, Alan Freed was working as a disc jockey in Cleveland, Ohio. Morris brought him to New York, and they began producing shows with multiple acts at the Brooklyn Paramount Theater. They were an instant success. Then Levy would sign those groups to Roulette Records. Freed then became the disc jockey for WINS, a radio station in New York that specialized in rock and roll at the time.

That term, by the way, rock and roll, was coined by Alan Freed.

Roulette was on its way with top artists like Frankie Lymon, Louie Lymon, Jimmie Rodgers, and in the 1960s, he scored big with Tommy James and Shondells.

At one point, Morris had told me he owned the publishing rights to a song called "A Thousand Miles Away." Another group recorded a song called "Daddy's Home" on another label. At the end of that song, they used the line, "You're not a thousand miles away." That turned out to be an infringement on Morris's song. He settled a lawsuit for the publishing rights to all the groups and their songs owned by the offending label. This put

Roulette Records over the top as far as cornering the market goes.

Levy then got into ownership of nightclubs like the Peppermint Lounge, the Round Table, and Birdland. He had a songwriter write "Lullaby of Birdland" for him, which became a timeless standard. All this success made him a target for the New York mob, who looked for ways to infiltrate the music industry.

Eventually, he got involved with my father, who gave him security and protection from others who would have jumped at the opportunity to get Levy and Roulette for themselves. Dad and Morris got along very well and soon began the business of selling cut-out records.

Promo Records, as it was called, did business out of a warehouse in Paterson, New Jersey, and was well on its way to becoming a success when Dad got killed.

When Promo Records started, Dad asked me to place a group life and health plan into effect for all the employees. I did this and created different levels of life insurance coverage for the executives and middle management and the working class. I placed the policy with a company that I had used many times, so I had a longstanding relationship with them.

When my father was killed, I put in a claim from my mother. She was a beneficiary for double indemnity as his death came as an accident. This meant that the company would have to pay double the coverage. Well, I got a call to come to their offices on William Street for a conference regarding the claim. They had no idea who my father was or that I was his son. I had given them a substantial amount of good business in the eight years I was an agent for them.

The purpose of this meeting was to inform me that they would pay the claim, but they were going to cancel my agency license with them and they no longer, obviously, would do business with me. In the end, I got them to agree not to cancel my license, but just let it stay, and I would never submit any new business to them again. Ironically, they were the first company that gave me a license.

Many years later, Tommy James published the story of his life. In that book, he explained how he hired auditors to review his financial transactions with Levy and Roulette Records. In the end, authorities determined that Levy had shorted Tommy James about $40 million.

It turns that Tommy James saw my father the day before he died. They met at the office of Roulette Records, and according to James, my father told him how proud everyone was of his success. It was a moment that James never forgot. The next night, James was playing a concert at Brooklyn's Paramount Theater, where Levy got his start, just a few blocks from where my father was killed.

Chapter 9

Vincent Gigante

Vincent "Chin" Gigante was in my life for as long as I can remember. My father managed his professional boxing career, and when Gigante stepped away from the ring, Dad took him under his wing on the streets.

Chin and Tony Pellone grew up together, and my father taught both of them how to box when they were still teenagers. They all had their roots in the West Village. If you look at photos from Tony's wedding, there is my father, the best man, and Gigante, as one of the groomsmen.

While Tony became the number one rated welterweight in the world, Chin never reached that level. Still, he had a respectable run in boxing. My father skillfully guided his career to a 21–4 record as a light heavyweight. When Tony beat contender LuLu Constantino at the Queensboro Arena in 1945, Gigante and future Hall of Famer Sandy Saddler were the main attractions. Gigante also fought at Madison Square Garden on Tony's undercards. In 1945, Chin scored a second-round knockout underneath the Willie Pep-Phil Terranova featherweight title fight at the Garden. Saddler also appeared on that card with Chin. Just a few years later, Saddler and Pep would engage in a dramatic four-fight series in which they traded the featherweight title back and forth.

Gigante decided to retire after getting stopped by Jimmy Slade in 1947. The

Gigante–Slade bout was the main event at the Ridgewood Grove Arena. Slade had a 10–1 record, and this fight was likely to send one of them toward a top ten ranking. Chin suffered a bad cut over his right eye, forcing the referee to stop the fight in the seventh round. Slade went on to fight Archie Moore and Floyd Patterson. Gigante would pursue far more dangerous endeavors.

*****

On the day of my confirmation, I was set to be confirmed by my Uncle Pat. But the priest informed Uncle Pat that he had to be confirmed first before he could confirm anyone else. At a moment's notice, Chin stepped in and confirmed him.

In the early 1950s, my mother and father stood as godparents to Vincent and Olympia's son, Andrew. In 1954, my father's sister

Rosemarie married Olympia's brother Emmy. That's how close our families were.

Everyone in the West Village was close at that time. My father, Uncle Pat, Vito Genovese, his brother Mike Genovese, Fat Dom Alongi, and all the Gigantes. Chin and Fat Dom were business partners as well as very close friends.

When I was in the insurance business and working in New York City, I would make it a point to stop by Chin's place, the Triangle Social Club, about once a month.

I was there having a cup of coffee one time in 1970. Chin was playing cards with four or five other guys in the back. All of a sudden, this character walks through the front door. He was an older man with a full Santa Claus–type beard. Somebody sitting by the door said, "Can I help you?"

The guy says, "I want to see Chin."

Chin looked up from the back table and shook his head no.

The guy at the door says, "What do you want to see him about?"

"I want to see him about buying some stuff" was the answer he gave.

Not in a million years would this guy get a chance to speak directly to Chin. So the guy at the door points to Fat Dom Alongi and says, "Okay, he's sitting right there, over in the corner."

The guy sits down at the table with Fat Dom. I was standing right there, I could hear all of this.

Fat Dom says, "What can I do for you? What do you want to buy?"

Fat Dom listens intently and then walks over to Gigante and says, "The guy wants to buy a couple of kilos of heroin. He wants to buy some cocaine, he wants to buy some marijuana."

Chin didn't waste any time. He got up and started beating the crap out of this guy. He punched the hell out of him. He missed a couple of shots and wound up punching the door. When it was over, his hand was all bloody.

Then Chin says to a couple of his guys, "Take this son of a bitch around the corner to MacDougal Street, go to one of the apartment buildings, put him under the stairway, and don't let him come out."

After the guy left, Chin just shook his head and said, "Can you believe that? This son of a bitch thought he was going to buy drugs in here."

Say what you want about guys like Chin or guys like my dad. But the neighborhood was safe in those days. Everyone respected the pecking order and the sanctity of the community. If people stepped out of line, they were dealt with, just like Santa Claus was in the Triangle.

*****

While researching this book, I was presented with FBI files that suggested there was a time when my father wanted to kill Chin, but Vito overruled him. According to the file, Chin was stealing money. I tend not to believe that because such an offense called for an automatic death penalty. As I've stated before, FBI files cannot be fully trusted, and I have never heard of any type of falling-out between my father and Chin. They were close for decades.

Vincent would eventually become boss of the Genovese family. It was well documented that he feigned dementia to avoid prosecution. Gigante would walk around the West Village in his bathrobe and mumble incoherently. The plan was brilliant. The claim was that Gigante suffered from a diminished capacity due to his boxing career. It worked for years.

The original idea of feigning illness may have come from my father.

It was around 1970, and my father was being called to testify before a New Jersey commission on organized crime. I was in the city, and I heard on the radio that my father had suffered a heart attack and was in the hospital. I drove to NYU Medical Center and went up to his room. My father had already had a serious heart attack, so I was nervous. I walked into the room, I approached the bed, and he winked at me. So right there, I said to myself, "Okay, I get it."

Is this where Chin came up with his idea? I don't know, but it's plausible.

*****

Several years ago, when I was living in Florida, I met Mario Gigante for dinner. He was Vincent's brother and was also a made member of the Genovese family. Over the course of dinner, he said to me, "We were all proud of the way you conducted yourself after your father died."

I knew what he meant. I didn't cause problems. I didn't make waves. We were all supposed to understand that this was the life they chose, and they knew more often than not, this is how it would end. The same way I told Tony Strollo's kid the day I ran into him after his father disappeared.

I may have acted the right way, but I was never okay with what happened. My father was a boss. That was not supposed to happen. Given his rising stature in the family, I believe that Chin knew. My father didn't deserve that. He made a lot of people a lot of money, including Chin.

That kind of betrayal is something I will never be okay with. It illustrates the callous, remorseless grind of organized crime. Every man is expendable; loyalty is a cliché, not a code. Loyalty only exists in the present; it goes only as far the whim of the next boss.

What a life.

Chapter 10

Louie and Tommy

My father may have been out of the fight game for a while, but he certainly still had his connections. It didn't matter how big the fight was, if my father wanted in, he was getting tickets. Such was the case for the first fight between Muhammad Ali and Joe Frazier on March 8, 1971, at Madison Square Garden. They were calling it "The Fight of the Century," and it was the hardest ticket to get in the entire country. That is, for most people. We were there. My father sat ringside with Morris Levy, and my brothers and I, along with some special guests, were about halfway up from the ring at the Garden.

I sat with my two brothers, Louie and Tommy, and some friends from Chicago: Jackie Cerone Jr., Tony Accardo Jr., and Paul DeLucia Jr. (Ricca). They all came to town just to see the fight. We went to dinner at Ponte's Restaurant on DeBrosses Street before the fight, and then afterward, I took them all to the Copacabana.

The match was a fifteen-round slugfest. Before the fight, my father told me about an adage in boxing that he would cite often. He said a shorter man always has the advantage over a taller man because the shorter man would be punching up and, therefore, be more effective. That's certainly what it looked like when Frazier put a beating on Ali that night. From where we were sitting, when Frazier knocked him down in the final round, it looked like Ali levitated. His legs came up to meet his body before he went crashing down to the canvas. The red tassels on his boxing shoes were flickering in the smoky air at the Garden.

It was a great night with great company. I always enjoyed spending time with my brothers.

*****

My brother Louie was born in Chicago and Tommy was born in New York, but they were both raised in Chicago. When the marriage between my father and Anna Ariola didn't work out, Anna, her mother, Louie, and Tommy all left New York and went back to the Windy City. The relationship between the Eboli family and the Ariolas dated back to prohibition when my grandfather was bootlegging across the Midwest and bringing my teenage father along for the ride. The Ariola family was well respected within the Chicago Outfit. Anna's brother, Chester, was the boss of Melrose Park and a close associate of Paul Ricca Sr. Chester's brother-in-law, Guido Di Chiaro, was also a top lieutenant for Ricca.

Ricca was a legend in the Chicago Outfit. It has been said that he once saved Al Capone's life. In 1926, Ricca was outside a restaurant when he saw a pair of sedans approaching at a high rate of speed. Sensing trouble, Ricca ran inside the restaurant, and just as the occupants of the vehicles began to open fire with machine guns, he called out for Capone to take cover. Although Ricca was shot in the arm, Capone was able to walk away from the incident unharmed. The two became good friends, and in 1927, Capone served as the best man at Ricca's wedding.

In 1931, when Capone went to prison, Ricca was elevated to underboss and eventually became the boss of Chicago. He would attend the national commission meetings that were organized by Lucky Luciano.

My brothers Louie and Tommy grew up under the guidance of their uncles Chester and Guido. By the time they reached their teens, they were picking up betting slips, relaying messages, and running errands for the outfit. Louie was right at home in this milieu. He was forging a career path in organized crime from an early age. Tommy, on the other hand, realized this life was not for him.

While I didn't meet Louie until I got out of the Marine Corps and made a trip to Chicago, I did meet Tommy when I was home on leave. Tommy had just graduated college, and he and a friend had driven east. His intention was to see Dad and meet me, my mother, and my sisters. We got along great and became good friends over the years.

*****

When Guido Di Chiaro retired, he handed everything over to Louie, including his jukebox and gambling empires. Another one of Louie's uncles, Sam "Big Sam" Ariola, was also a mentor to my brother. Although not as powerful as Chester and Guido, Big Sam was on the streets with Louie. In 1962, Big Sam and Louie were arrested on charges of beating a man with a baseball bat.

The prosecutors claimed Sam hatched the plan and supervised while Louie issued the beating. Two police officers were also charged, prosecutors claiming that they looked the other way during the beef. The alleged victim was rigging pinball machines owned by the outfit. Sam and Louie were eventually found not guilty at trial, where a local politician testified on their behalf. On the witness stand, the Village President from their Franklin Park neighborhood described Ariola as a man with a very good reputation and called Louie, who was twenty-eight at the time, "a nice young fellow."

Louie picked up the nickname "Louie the Mooch." They said on the streets that the name evolved because he sometimes didn't make good on bets while he was a bookmaker. I happen to know that this nickname began back in his school days when he was always "mooching" food off his classmates.

Sam Ariola would make headlines a few years later when police confiscated $38,000 in cash and a phone book from his apartment. The phone book contained the unlisted numbers of numerous local politicians and a detective.

*****

My brother Tommy introduced me to big-game hunting in 1970. We made three or four trips to Wyoming, and he had a lot more success than I did. He shot a couple of nice elk, a black bear, a mountain lion, and antelope. Then in 1972, four months after our father's death, we gathered a group of friends and went to Douglas, Wyoming, on an antelope hunt. We stayed at a hunting lodge where the owner picked up on our last names and called in the local police. The police then notified the FBI. Our hunting party was similar to the group at the Ali–Frazier fight. It consisted of me, Thomas Eboli Jr., Tony Accardo Jr., and Jackie Cerone Jr. Steve Crea, who would eventually become the underboss of the Lucchese family, was also on the trip.

The Feds were disappointed to learn that we were all legitimate businessmen there to hunt. This was not some new generation Appalachian meeting. We all got a laugh out of it. When we were together, we never spoke about our fathers or the Life, we all just enjoyed each other's company.

From Douglas, we drove up to Yellowstone Park where we went back into the Absaroka Range for elk. Our outfitter was a man named Jerry Acey, who also had four or five of the astronauts in his camp. I remember the names of two of them, Deke Slayton and Jack Swigert. We all got along great, and it was a memorable trip.

When it was over, we started our drive home and heard on the radio that Paul Ricca Sr. had passed away. As soon as I got back to New York, I checked in with my Uncle Pat, and we decided that I should go back to Chicago for the funeral. At the funeral parlor, I met most of the hierarchy of the Chicago Outfit, who all offered their condolences for the recent loss of my father.

Louie eventually rose to a position of power and established himself as the number 3 man in all of Chicago. It's been widely reported that he was present for the hit on the Spilotro brothers, a scene that was memorialized in a cornfield at the end of the hit movie, *Casino*. If true, that's a pretty good indication of how important Louie was.

Tommy built a restaurant supply business that was substantial, to say the least. But he was putting in a lot of hours just to keep the business going and was looking for a change. Dad had invited Tommy to come to New Jersey and get involved in Promo Records as a minority partner, specializing in sales. Tommy was so successful at it that by 1971, he sold the restaurant supply business and began a new career in the cut-out record industry. Tommy was living with me while he was learning the business.

But about four months after Dad died, he went back to Chicago. Tommy saw things that I wasn't privy to and understood that it was just a matter of time before the Wiseguys took over Dad's cut-out record business. Tommy never shared with me any of that information. But when it was suggested to Morris Levy that they buy out Dad's percentage of the business, his response was "The business isn't worth anything. There's nothing to buy out, the entire business is in debt."

We knew that was not true.

When Tommy got back to Chicago, he went into the commercial real estate business.

The company he started managed buildings, bought and sold empty lots, and built and kept properties in the Bensenville and Franklin Park areas.

Louie passed away in 1987 from pancreatic cancer. A decade later, Tommy also passed away as a result of pancreatic cancer. Their mother, Anna, died in 2013 at the age of 101.

Chapter 11

The End of an Era

In 1970, I met my mother and father at JFK Airport. I was picking them up after a trip to Italy. They were going through customs, and when my father saw me, he got very sorrowful. He began crying.

"My father died, he's dead. He's gone. He's gone."

My grandfather Luigi had died during their visit to Italy. Luigi's death hit my father harder than I expected. There were two reasons I was surprised. The first was that I rarely saw him show any emotion. The second was that he would often be very critical of his father. But he was very, very emotional when he saw me. It showed me, no matter what twist and turns their relationship took over the years, the father-son bond is powerful.

Within two years, I found myself in the very same position.

In March of 1972, Crazy Joe Gallo, a well-known member of the Colombo family, was gunned down in Umberto's Clam House on Mulberry Street in Little Italy. He was celebrating his forty-third birthday with a small group of people when gunmen entered the restaurant at 4:30 a.m. and killed him. Dad was at my house a few days later, and we were watching the news on television. They were giving this murder a lot of coverage on television because of Gallo's notoriety.

I asked Dad, "Was this an isolated incident, or was there more to come?"

He answered, "This was only the beginning. There will be a lot more by the end of the year."

How prophetic.

The next month, I was at my father's apartment, and he told me that he wanted to make me aware that he might be implicated in a narcotics investigation. He told me that it was a frame-up, but explained that if he was convicted, he could be facing up to twenty-five years in prison.

My response was a portent of things to come.

I said, "How many guys make it to the top and either die in jail or get killed?" It was a rhetorical question. I didn't expect nor did I get an answer.

I never knew my father to be involved in drugs. Dealing in narcotics had always been a no-no for his people. So I am comfortable with him telling me that these charges were a frame-up. There was precedent for such a frame. In his book, *The Last Testament of Lucky Luciano*, Luciano described how he, Frank Costello, Carlo Gambino, and Meyer Lansky framed Vito Genovese for narcotics distribution in 1959. According to Luciano's book, this was payback for Genovese's attempt to kill Costello. Luciano and his group bribed a known drug dealer to set up Vito and testify against him in open court. This alleged "investigation" included a number of Vito's associates. When it was over, Genovese would be sentenced to fifteen years in federal prison, and he died while in custody in 1969. Vincent Gigante was caught up in the deception and was sentenced to seven years.

I remember during that time, my father would tell my mother, "Vito is getting framed."

Nonetheless, my father stepped into the power vacuum left by Genovese's prison sentence. It was very possibly, the beginning of the end.

At home, my father didn't talk much about what he did. Throughout his life, he didn't talk about his involvement in the Mafia. I never heard him use that word or Cosa Nostra. I'd occasionally overhear him talking to my mother about someone. I certainly suspected certain things over the years. When your dad sends you to meet Lucky Luciano, you start to wonder.

In around June of 1968, Dad had his first heart attack and was in the hospital for about a month. He was at home recuperating for quite a while and thought about retiring. But he was talked out of it by his associates because they felt he was too important to this organization.

He never threw his weight around with words. But he did have the ability to scare you to death. If he lost his temper, he would go right into action. Perhaps his temper may have been part of his downfall. He demanded loyalty from his people, and if they disappointed him, he would let them know it.

In the months before his demise, there were occasions when he would gather his associates at various locations and question why they were going to the East Side to meet with other capos. When the answers did not satisfy him, he would launch into a tirade about their loyalty to him. He should have seen what was coming.

At around this time, he sent for my brother Louie in Chicago. Louie was my half brother from my father's first marriage. He would eventually rise to the number 3 man in the Chicago Outfit. I picked Louie up at the airport, and I drove him to my father's house.

They moved into a different car, and my father stopped and said to me, "Do you want to ride with us?"

This was very unusual. But of course, I said, "Yes."

I never expected them to talk in front of me. This is a conversation that I have never repeated until now.

My father told Louie, "I am having big problems over here. There is no respect for Vito. There is no respect for what Vito stood for anymore. These guys want to do things that I don't want to do. It could come down to a showdown."

Louie said he would go back and speak to Tony Accardo, who was the boss of Chicago.

*****

On July 15, 1972, my father stopped by my house to meet his youngest grandson, Philip. My wife had given birth in late June, and this was the first time my father saw the baby. My father would often wear newsboy caps, and that day, he told me that he was going to purchase two of those hats for my older sons. He left for the city, and that was the last time I ever saw him.

My phone rang at five the next morning. It was my sister, who told me that Dad had been shot. I did not yet know that he was killed. His long-time driver, GI Joe Sternfeld left the scene of the shooting and drove my father's car straight to my sister's house in Westwood. I always wondered why he didn't just come to my house, which was closer. When the shooters approached my father's car, GI Joe laid down on the front seat. One of the shots blew out the driver's side window, and the shattered glass landed on him. She spent the night picking shards of glass out of GI Joe's back.

I turned on the television to search for an early news show, hoping against hope that nothing serious happened. But that was not to be. It was the lead story. Yes, he was dead. He was shot five times in the head. I immediately sank into a feeling of despair. But I had to force myself back into the reality of what happened. I had to figure out what I should to do next. I called my brothers in Chicago to alert them, in case they might also be in danger. I spoke to Tommy and then to Louie. They both said they would be on the first flight they could get, and they would call back with the flight information so I could pick them up at Newark Airport.

Next, I tried to get in touch with my Uncle Pat, but he was out on his boat for the weekend. I then called my Aunt Nancy, my father's youngest sister, who was only four years older than me. She lived close by, and I asked her husband Frank to drive me to the police precinct in Brooklyn to see if I could get more information on what had happened.

The police, of course, did not have anything to say other than that my father was dead and they had no idea who did it. They told me he was in the morgue at Kings County Hospital and that I should go there to identify my father's body.

My father's cousin, Pat Mucerino, lived in Ozone Park, not far from where we were. So we went to his house and had him come with us to the hospital. When we got there, we were directed to the basement where the morgue was. They had us wait in the hallway while they brought his body to the viewing area. It was behind a large glass window with drapes, which they opened when they had him positioned for viewing.

We acknowledged to them that it was my father. We advised the attendants that we would have the Romanelli Funeral Parlor pick him up as soon as possible. After that, I felt drained, but I knew I had to keep my wits about me and to be careful with whom I spoke and what I said.

At that time, I had no idea if, whoever did this, had any further plans for more bloodshed.

I was glad when my brothers arrived, so we could put our heads together and think all of this through.

The funeral mass was at St. Anthony's on Sullivan Street. They didn't want to do the mass at first, but my Uncle Pat went to see the priest. He said that this has always been my father's home parish and that my father had always given his support to St. Anthony's. Each year, he had a mass said for his mother here.

"I can tell you right now that he will be buried out of this church, whether you like it or not," my Uncle Pat told the priest. "And if you don't do it, you will not be supported by me and my friends."

The mass was at St. Anthony's and was presided over by Father Louis Gigante, Chin's brother.

Whoever killed my father was never caught. To this day, his murder remains an unsolved mystery. I believe men close to him probably made a pitch to the powers that be that my dad was sick and not taking care of the things that needed to be done. That it was time for a change. History tells us that the perpetrators usually will be the replacements.

And if that's the case, his own men could be guilty. But who is to say? I don't have any proof that this is what actually happened.

What I do know is that they took his street businesses and the money associated with it for themselves. My Uncle Pat told me this.

One night about two months after my father was killed, a friend of Dad's showed up at my house with a package of money for my mother, telling me that every so often, as my father's money was collected, he would bring her more. He never came back again. It was like that old saying, "To the victor goes the spoils." That was not uncommon in the Life. But if you promise the widow money, you should stick to your word.

Dad and Morris Levy were partners in the cut-out record industry and had a warehouse in Paterson, New Jersey. My father actually spent a lot of time there, and the business was thriving.

After my father's death, the new boss sent a message that they would put my mother on the payroll and she would have an income. Considering that this was a legitimate business, I couldn't understand how these men of honor could take it, but they did. My mother got exactly one payroll check.

When this happened, I went up to Morris Levy's office to ask why. He told me it wasn't his doing and that if I wanted to know why, I should go see Vincent Gigante. Morris now belonged to Chin, and he took his orders from him.

So my mother never saw another dime from Dad's businesses. Fortunately, she had social security and the dividends from some stock that they owned in AT&T. She finally made a lot of money some twelve years later when AT&T was ordered to divest itself, and it became seven companies, The value of these companies began to skyrocket, and my mother lived comfortably for the rest of her life.

In addition to the trauma of losing a father and a husband who controlled our lives, we now found that we had to make our own decisions. I learned to live without someone who could get things done with the snap of a finger. It was a real awakening to be on our own without a leader. We all had to reconcile ourselves to the fact that life without my father was going to be a challenge.

Several months after my father died, the police released the contents of Dad's pockets, which included all of his personal possessions: his glasses, watch, wallet, and the two hats he had purchased for my sons.

Louie did not yet talk to Tony Accardo because he was on a fishing trip. By the time he had gotten back, it was too late.

*****

GI Joe was a longtime, loyal employee of my father. He got the nickname GI Joe because he served in the United States Army during World War II. He also operated a pushcart business in the Village called GI Joe's Frankfurters. He would put American flags all over the cart. He was around my father for nearly two decades. He drove my father around and would make trips to the store and pick things up for him. Every year, he put up the Christmas lights at my father's house.

Here's an example of GI Joe's loyalty. When Vito Genovese was in Italy during World War II, he had a relationship with a German woman named Charlotte and she had a daughter by Vito. Being the obedient person that GI Joe was, they sent him to Italy to marry Charlotte just so she and Vito's daughter could come to the United States. He did just that, no questions asked. Vito's daughter, Isabella, arrived a week before I left for the Marine Corps. She did not speak a word of English but enrolled at St. Cecilia's High School in Englewood, New Jersey, the same school my sisters went to. After that, she attended Georgetown University and, upon graduation, became a translator at the United Nations.

After my father's death, I had asked GI Joe to come over and string up the Christmas lights. He declined.

I said, "What, you would do this for my father, but not for me?"

He explained that some of the shrubs around the house gave him an allergic reaction, and that each year, after stringing the lights, he would break out severely. But no matter what, he'd always do that for my father.

Loyalty aside, I had some reservations about GI Joe driving Dad. I felt that my father should have had better bodyguards. A man in his position needed better protection. I had always heard that GI Joe was good with his hands, but to my knowledge, he never carried a gun.

In the news accounts of the time and in FBI reports, my father had been described in numerous ways—boss of the Genovese family, acting boss, and street boss. I believe that my father had always felt that he was the boss of the family. But after his death, my Uncle Pat and I were talking about that. He said that, in truth, Philip "Benny Squint" Lombardo was the boss. My Uncle Pat told me that he was in the room when Vito made him the boss just before he went to prison.

In addition to this, Uncle Pat had once asked Dad, "If you're the boss, how come you report to Benny every Tuesday night and how come you help him put his coat on when he leaves? The fact of the matter is, you are a capo regime and not the boss."

I believe that Dad's ego may have led him to think he was the boss because he was in charge on the street. He may very well have been the front boss, the guy with all the exposure.

My Uncle Pat had always been my father's right-hand man and wielded substantial power. But suddenly, with the death of my father, he was broken, as he said, "from a lieutenant colonel to a corporal." He had nobody and felt that it was only a matter of time before they came for him.

As a kid, there were times when I honestly wished that Uncle Pat was my father. I had such a good relationship with him. I was thrilled every time he came up to Greenwood Lake. He used to take me places; we were always going somewhere.

"Come on, come on, get in the car. Take a ride with me."

It was my Uncle Pat who confirmed me. But the interesting story about that day was Uncle Pat never made his confirmation. According to the church, you cannot confirm someone if you are not confirmed. So that same day, Vincent Gigante confirmed my Uncle Pat. I would eventually confirm his son Tommy, who is ten years younger than me.

My Uncle Pat was very diplomatic. He was a hot-tempered guy, but he balanced it with diplomacy when the situation called for it. He never flaunted who he was. He did a lot of socializing with people that you wouldn't expect him to socialize with. Lawyers, big business people. They were all legitimate people. My father used to kid him and say to him, "Just don't forget where you came from."

That was, of course, a joke between brothers. But in the Life, no one ever forgets. My Uncle Pat knew he always had a target on his back.

*****

On June 1, 1976, my Uncle Pat stopped by his son Tommy's house to see his new grandson and namesake. When he left to go into the city, he was going to meet his fate. His car was found a month later in a long-term parking lot at JFK Airport. The car was wiped clean of prints, and it was not damaged in any way. Uncle Pat's prints were not even found on the car.

When he had finally reached a certain level of comfort, he disappeared, never to be heard from again.

My cousin called me three days after Uncle Pat disappeared and asked if I can find anything out. The next day, I went downtown to see if perhaps he had been sent somewhere on business or if they knew where he was. I talked to Fat Dom Alongi and Mario Gigante. Their responses were textbook denial of any knowledge about my uncle's whereabouts. They both said they had no idea where he was and didn't even know he was out of town.

Mario said, "I talk to you like you're one of the guys. Believe me when I tell you, because we don't know anything about this."

It should be noted here that after Dad's death, my uncle told me emphatically to stay away from downtown. He did not want me talking to anybody down there. He never gave a reason, but he made it clear to me that I was not to go there.

After speaking with Fat Dom and Mario, I then went to Vincent Gigante's apartment on Sullivan Street. The first question he asked me was why I hadn't been there to see him since my father died.

I explained to him that my uncle asked me not to go downtown because he was concerned that I might say the wrong thing or ask questions that I shouldn't.

Gigante said, "You could come here anytime you want. You come right to me. Come on, let's sit over here. You can ask me anything you want, and I'll tell you the truth. Shoot."

I asked him about my Uncle Pat and he said he did not know where he was.

So I then asked him why a man of my father's stature should be shot down in the gutter the way he was? Why wasn't he just made to retire?

His answer was astounding.

He said that I should be happy that I have a grave to go to, not like my aunt and cousins who don't know what happened to their father or husband.

When I heard this pearl of wisdom, I knew it was time to go and not ask any more questions.

It all had a devastating effect on me because it was the end of an era.

Chapter 12

Legacy

The death of my father was deeply traumatic on a personal level. I would soon come to realize its financial impact. I had built a very successful insurance agency. There were many clients who were directed my way by my father and his attorneys. When I realized that I wasn't going to be getting any more business from those sources, it would present a hardship that would take years to overcome. With young children to take care of, I had to make a decision. So I decided to sell the agency. One of the purchasers of the business was the son-in-law of a capo from the Genovese family in Brooklyn. I sold it to him and his partner.

In discussing the terms of sale, the offer was a little less than what I had hoped for, so my Uncle Pat had discussed a better deal with Fat Dom Alongi. Fat Dom was acting as a go-between to get this deal done. On the occasion when I went downtown to inquire about my uncle's disappearance, I asked Fat Dom if the more favorable contract had been accepted by them. He said, "Yes, they agreed to my terms."

I told Fat Dom that it was a shame that I had to sell this business. I thought that I had done a good job of handling it over the last seven or eight years. I told him that I didn't understand why I was not going to get any more business.

He said, "The same way you got these accounts, that's how you lose them. They go to someone else now. You gotta understand there are new people in charge now, and they want to give the insurance to somebody else. They want to give it to their son or their nephew or their niece. Or whoever. You have to expect these things are gonna happen. That's just the way it is."

As you can see, the loss of my father impacted my life on every level.

*****

There were times that Dad performed what would be commonly called good deeds, but to him, they were natural responses to someone's immediate needs. He never talked or bragged about helping others. It was not in his nature. Needless to say, these events were never reported in the press or the hundreds of pages that the FBI kept on my dad.

One such deed that I witnessed was in 1967 at a barber shop on Thompson Street about two weeks before Thanksgiving. My father was getting his haircut and talking to Vincent Gigante. I was waiting next in line to get my hair cut. Dad told Chin to bring him $20,000 in $20 bills. He decided that anyone who came into Cafe Napoli di Notte to wish him a Happy Thanksgiving would be given $20 to buy a turkey. Chin was flabbergasted by the gesture. I was pleasantly surprised.

This was my father's way of showing kindness to the local residents, who walked the same street as he did and whom he cared about very much.

Another act of kindness occurred shortly before he was killed. He went to the hospital to visit a friend, Domenic Crea, who was recovering from heart surgery. Crea told me this story after my father had died.

When my father was on the elevator, it stopped on a particular floor, and when it opened, he saw numerous children playing in the hall. He asked a nurse why they were all playing in the hallway. She responded by saying that they were waiting for treatment on a kidney dialysis machine. The nurse went on to explain that there was only one dialysis machine in the hospital, so all the kids had to spend hours there while they waited their turn. My father put out word to many of his friends in the Life, and they raised enough money to purchase two more dialysis machines for the hospital. The responses from his associates were enthusiastic and generous, and the hospital got the message.

There were some lighter moments in his stressful life, such as the time in 1962 when he was awarded an oversized golf club with a very crooked shaft, by the members of the Englewood Gold Club. This was because he often broke his own clubs in frustration while on the golf course. This humorous event took place at the end-of-season banquet and was enjoyed by the entire membership of the club.

Another such event took place on the night of my parent's twenty-fifth wedding anniversary.

After a wonderful dinner party at a fine Italian restaurant in Hillsdale, New Jersey, it was on to the Copacabana in New York for drinks and dancing. We were in the lounge, and it wasn't very crowded, so we had plenty of room to dance. When my father started doing the twist, the entire staff of waiters, busboys, and captains broke out in applause because they never expected this from him. They only knew Thomas Eboli as the mobster, as the man who really was the boss of the Copacabana.

The Englewood Golf Club was a place where both me and my father enjoyed some good times. The club is well over a century old and has a pretty impressive history. It initially opened as a nine-hole course in 1896; a second nine was added four years later. It actually hosted the US Amateur in 1906 and the US Open in 1909.

In the mid-1960s, it became very popular among celebrities. Willie Mays came out to the Englewood Golf Club. A lot of the Yankees used to come there to play golf; Mickey Mantle used to play there regularly. The pitcher Ralph Terry was another one who was there often.

The comedian Buddy Hackett was a regular at the club. He lived right on the golf course; he had a house on the seventh hole. I used to play with him regularly. One time, Buddy and I were partners, and we were playing a $10 Nassau against Dick Martin from *Rowan and Martin* and Don Adams from *Get Smart*.

The eighteenth hole was a semi-short par 4, about 235 yards or 240 yards. It had an elevated green with sand traps all along the front and very thick grass in between the traps. I hit my drive into this heavy thick grass, and I really had no shot. I looked at every possibility, but I saw no way to get the ball onto the green. So I moved the ball out of the thick grass.

Buddy comes over to me after I hit my shot onto the green, and he said to me, "You know, they saw you move the ball, now we have to forfeit the hole and you just cost me $10."

I said, "Buddy, you want the $10? Here, take it. I had no shot at all, so I took a chance, and I moved the ball."

"Well," said Buddy, "they saw you."

If I was anybody else, he would have thrown a temper tantrum.

Buddy was a pretty good golfer, but he had a terrible temper. Anyone who played with him had to be very quiet and still. If they weren't, he would tear into them as if they were intentionally trying to distract him or throw off his game. Anyone, except me. He would be very nice to me and was very pleasant to play with simply because of my father.

If we had a game arranged, he would always suck up to Dad, telling him, "Hi, Tommy, I'm playing with your son today."

My father used to be hysterical over that. In response, my father would tell him, "Just don't get mad out on the course."

Another good deed of my dad's occurred on this very golf course, but it also landed him in the hospital. He had his own golf cart, so he never had to rent one. It happened to be a three-wheel cart, which could be dangerous if you were not careful. One day while playing, there were these two women playing just ahead of him. They lost control of their cart, going downhill. They were yelling for help and were afraid they would crash. So my father started racing toward them in an effort to stop the runaway cart. Suddenly, he lost control of his own cart. His cart turned over, and he went flying. Dad ended up with a broken left leg and a fractured right shoulder and a brief stay in the hospital.

This cart happened to be a gift to him from Frank Erickson. Frank was once Arnold Rothstein's right-hand man and was known as one of the biggest bookmakers in the country. He gave me my first wedding envelope. It was just a plain white envelope, no card inside of it. It simply had "TR" written across the front of the envelope. It contained $500.

This cart was also equipped with a radio. Whenever people were playing slowly in front of us, Dad would turn that radio up, full blast. It was a not-so-subtle reminder to play at a quicker pace.

*****

As you have read on these pages, my relationship with my father was tumultuous. It may not have been the perfect childhood, and it was certainly not how I raised my sons.

But I am unequivocally proud that Tomasso Vito Eboli was my father.

In the very first sentence of this book, I wrote that he was a complicated man. He was indeed that. My father was committed to the Life. There were surely other Wiseguys *as* committed, but I believe that it can be said that no one was *more* committed. He took the oath and never wavered. In many ways, that cost us. Upon entrance into the Mafia, you swear that everyone and everything is second to the Family—and that includes your biological family. The rules were not open to interpretation; there were no loopholes. The Genovese family came first. We lost precious time with our father. He was often absent from the biggest moments and events in our lives. His business hours were not conducive to raising a family.

Time is not all we lost.

I never heard my father tell me that he loved me. But I am certain that he did. I was never more sure of this as when he greeted me after I came home from the Marines on my first leave. Or when I picked him up at the airport after his own father died.

As a parent, I know and understand that the love of a child is absolute and unconditional. My father's life, though, was always bound by certain conditions. Those conditions, in place for decades, were the foundation of an empire in which he flourished. It left little room for anything else. Perhaps he steeled himself from submitting to parental emotions, knowing that it could all disappear in an instant. That's only speculation on my part. I do believe he felt strongly for us, that we held a greater place in his heart than he let on. I think it's reasonable to assume that a man who valued loyalty above most things was, at the very least, loyal to us.

My father once told me, shortly after I got out of the Marines, that I should always be humble. That he lived a humble existence and that was one of the reasons behind his success. He told me that he had the power to stop every truck in the United States at a given moment. That's power.

My father was, as they say in that Life, a man of honor. He commanded enough respect from his family members that many Ebolis named their sons after him.

There's my son, Tommy. His son (my grandson) is named Tommy. Then there's my cousin Tommy. My cousin Tommy also has a grandson named Tommy. There was my brother Tommy. And he had a son named Tommy. He had another son named James, who has a son named Tommy, whom we call TJ.

In a very real way, Tommy Eboli lives on. That is quite a legacy.

Even today some fifty-two years after his death, the pain of losing my father is in my heart. I cannot begin to describe how his untimely demise has affected my life. I thought perhaps writing this book would help me forget, but it has only brought back the haunting memories of his tragic life. Not a day goes by that I don't think about what could have been. I will miss him until the day I die.

The Cast of Characters

Madeline Eboli: My sister, eighteen months older than me. Madeline always wanted to be a teacher. When we were kids, she would sit me down and pretend I was her student. She always got straight As in school. She received a scholarship to the College of Mt. St. Vincent. My father would allow her to only attend an all-girls college. But when she got a full scholarship to Purdue for her master's degree, my father balked at first because it was co-ed. But he couldn't stop her because it was free. When her children were old enough, she began to teach mathematics at a local junior college. She retired after thirty years.

Maryann Eboli: My sister Maryann was also an excellent student, but when my father insisted that she go to an all-girls school, she declined and missed out on the college experience. She went to secretarial school for a year, specializing in bookkeeping. She developed into a successful assistant, working with Leona Helmsley and Ralph Lauren and his partner, Peter Strom. She is still active, working with a select clientele.

Thomas Eboli a.k.a. Tommy Ryan: A controlling dad who was the street boss of the Genovese family. We had a tumultuous relationship, but we grew closer as a I got older.

Pasquale Eboli, a.k.a. Pat Ryan: Pat was always my favorite uncle. We didn't get to know each other until after the war, when he got out of the army. Once we got to know each other, it developed into a great relationship. He, of course, was a member of the Genovese family. He became my father's right-hand man and someone he could trust.

Vincent "Chin" Gigante: A protégé of my dad's, first in the boxing ring and later in the Life. Vincent was around our family since the time I was a young kid. In fact, he was there the day I was confirmed. He had a brief pro boxing career and then rose through the ranks of the Genovese family. He would ultimately become boss of the family.

Vito Genovese: An original member of Lucky Luciano's crime syndicate, Vito would become boss of the family that still bears his name today. My father always spoke highly of Vito and had a tremendous amount of respect for him. Dad looked at Vito as a barometer for what a Wiseguy should be like. I only met Vito once, when I was twelve years old. He came to the house one day. I had no idea who he was. When my father introduced me to him, he told me, "This is your Uncle Vito." Once he said that, I knew this was a man I should respect.

Charles "Lucky" Luciano: The architect of modern-day organized crime. When

I first met Charlie in Naples, Italy, I knew that I was in the presence of greatness. What I didn't know was what he meant to my father and Uncle Pat. He treated me as if I was his own son. Over a six-month period, we spent many hours talking about what I wanted to do when I got out of the Marines. We had a terrific time together and especially with Dad when he came over for New Year's Eve.

"Tough" Tony Pellone: He rose to a number one ranking in the welterweight division while the great Sugar Ray Robinson was champion. Tony fought and beat some of the best fighters in the world and, at one time, held the record for the most main events fought at Madison Square Garden. My father discovered him shining shoes on the streets of the West Village. I was young, six, seven, eight years old when Tony used to live with us in Greenwood Lake. What I remember most about him was his dedication to boxing and his willingness to sacrifice for excellence in the ring.

Rocky Castellani: A former Marine, Rocky became a top middleweight contender who would eventually challenge for the title. He would also engage in a memorable bout with Robinson. I spent more time with Rocky because I was a little bit older when he stayed with us. I would run with him in the mornings and take walks with him in the evening. I would also go to Stillman's Gym with him and watch him train. Like Tony Pellone, he was dedicated to his sport and, like Tony, trusted my father implicitly.

Bert Berns: Bert and my father were more than just business associates; they were good friends. They enjoyed each other's company, and they loved boating together. In his short life, Bert wrote over five hundred songs and fifty-one became top ten hits. His wife told me that on New Year's Eve, he came home and said, "I am going to lay down for a while." He never woke up. Among his many hits were "Twist and Shout" and "Piece of My Heart."

Morris Levy, Roulette Records: I knew Morris through Dad, and we got along nicely. In fact, my brother-in-law and I spent a weekend deer hunting at his farm in upstate New York. He was very personable, but I've heard he also had a very bad temper. He also had a habit of not wanting to pay his artists or his bills, unless it was absolutely necessary.

Tommy James and the Shondells: In his book, *Me, the Mob and the Music*, James speaks highly of my father. If you read the book, you can also understand why he would want to get away from Morris Levy. A movie will be made of the book in 2024

Louis Eboli and Thomas Eboli Jr.: My half brothers from Dad's first marriage. They both grew up in Melrose Park, Illinois, under the guidance of their uncles, Chester and Guido. They became very successful in their chosen fields of endeavor.

Luigi Eboli: Luigi was my grandfather. He came to America as a stowaway, and he met Vito Genovese while they were both passengers in steerage. Luigi desperately wanted to be a part of the mob. When they did not accept him, he said, "Then take my son." Thus, my father's life was chosen for him.

Paul DeLucia (Ricca) a.k.a. Paul the Waiter: He was the right-hand man and successor to Al Capone. He and my father were very good friends. In fact, Paul and his wife were best man and maid of honor when Dad married Anna.

Philip Lombardo a.k.a. Benny Squint: He became the boss of the Genovese family when Vito went to jail in 1959. He made my father the underboss or street boss until my father's death in 1972. Benny Squint did a fantastic job of staying in the shadows until he retired to Florida around 1980. He died peacefully in 1981.

Photos

Here's a collection of family photos that have never been seen before:

Xavier Eboli, on leave, with his parents, top, portrait of Marine, bottom

Philip Eboli

The Eboli children

A young Thomas Eboli, left, approximately sixteen years old. On right with boxer Tony Pellone and trainer Baby Saban.

Thomas Eboli, left, Pasquale Eboli, center, Vincent Gigante, right, the day Xavier Eboli was confirmed

Genovese Capo Fat Dom Alongi, Lou Costello, Thomas Eboli

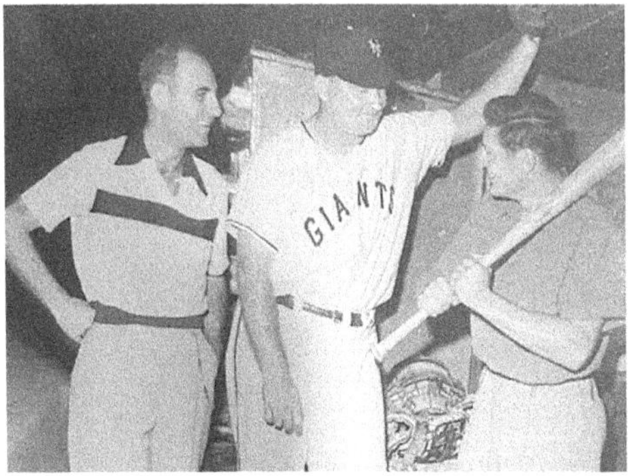

Thomas Eboli, baseball Hall of Famer
Johnny Mize, Rocky Castellani

A golden boxing glove presented to Tommy Ryan
from his former fighter, Wayland Douglas

Award for “most golf clubs broken”

Throughout his public life, Eboli was a fixture in the headlines of the day.

Commission To Hear Eboli

By EDWARD NORTON
Staff Writer

NEW YORK—Reputed racketeer Thomas "Tommy Ryan" Eboli of Fort Lee is among those called to testify before the bistate Waterfront Commission anticrime hearings that begin today.

The commission plans to question many reputed crime family leaders who have links through businesses or unions to the New York-New Jersey docks.

The commission until late yesterday had been unable to serve Eboli with a subpoena. The tempermental, 60-year-old mob figure lives at 4 Horizon House, Fort Lee. He was served with a subpoena by commission agents yesterday as he stepped off the liner France following a cruise.

Eboli and two other Bergen

EBOLI GIGANTE
A Date To Testify

eree after a bout his boxer lost.

The commission seeks to uncover the lines of control for waterfront gambling, thefts, and loansharking.

Others scheduled to appear before the commission today and tomorrow are:

• Vincent "The Chin" Gigante of Old Tappan, a convicted heroin dealer who was indicted last year by a Bergen County jury for alleged payoffs to Old Tappan police. Gigante in 1970 identified himself as a $300-a-week dispatcher for a Bronx trucking firm.

• Eli Zeccardi, 61, of 266 Audubon Road, Englewood, a co-owner of the Cafe Roma on Broome Street in lower Manhattan. The FBI has identified Zeccardi as a member of the Genovese-Eboli crime family.

• Michael Clemente of Manhattan, a former official in the International Longshoreman's Association.

• Saro Mogavero, a convicted extortionist, and former union official with ties to the waterfront.

"We haven't reached the position of bringing definite charges against these men," said a spokesman for the commission.

Information from the investigation could be used during public hearings by the quasi-judicial bistate agency.

Morgenthau Accuses One-Time Manager of Rocky Castellani

Eboli Is Labeled Top Crime Ring Figure

Thomas (Tommy Ryan) Eboli

By TOM CASEY

A man who managed ex-fighter Attilio (Rocky) Castellani has been named as one of the top figures in organized crime in New York and New Jersey.

U.S. Atty. Robert M. Morgenthau of New York City told United Press International that Thomas "Tommy Ryan" Eboli, 53, Englewood Cliffs, N.J., is one of six men under investigation for allegedly infiltrating legitimate businesses in New York and New Jersey.

Eboli was Castellani's manager when the Luzerne County middleweight advanced to the top of his class in the mid 50's.

Castellani, 39, a native of Luzerne, currently operates a restaurant in Atlantic City, N.J.

Castellani lost a 15 round decision to Carl (Bobo) Olson for the world middleweight championship Aug. 31, 1954. He engaged in at least 17 bouts in Scranton.

Among his opponents in this city were Jiggs Donahoe, Billy Kilroy, Terry Moore, Joey Giardello (whom he decisioned in 10 rounds), Gene Hairston, Harold Green, Lenny (Boom Boom) Mancini, Tony Janiro and Gene Boland. Castellani also took part in numerous bouts in Wilkes-Barre.

Eboli was barred from boxing some years ago.

Morgenthau told UPI that mobsters have moved into the meat industry, the stock market, labor unions and the small loans business.

Prime targets of the investigation, in addition to Eboli, are:

Thomas "Three Finger Brown" Lucchese, 64, Lido Beach, L.I.

Gerald Catena, 63, South Orange, N.J.

Carlo Gambino, 53, 2230 Ocean Parkway, Brooklyn.

Joseph Anthony Colombo, 40, 1460 77th St., Brooklyn.

Frank LaBruzzo, 53, Bellerose Manor, Queens, N.Y.

Morgenthau said he is convinced that Vito Genovese, behind prison bars for a federal narcotics conviction, is still giving orders to some lieutenants on the outside—chiefly Eboli.

Eboli, according to Morgenthau, is suspected of some stock market manipulations. He also owns a trucking business.

Castellani, according to The Ring record book, began his professional career by using the name Rocky Wargo. He fought six fights under that name and first used his correct name in a six-round bout with Carbondale's Paulie Wilson in this city Feb. 14, 1944. The bout was a draw.

Eboli was barred from boxing following an incident in the Castellani-Ernie Durando bout of Jan. 11, 1952.

Durando was declared a winner by a technical knockout in the seventh round.

Eboli, infuriated by the call, jumped into the ring and attacked the referee, Ray Miller.

Later, he assaulted Al Weill, the Madison Square Garden matchmaker.

Eboli was given a lifetime suspension by the New York State Athletic Commission.

Rocky Comments

From BOB CHRISTENBERRY to TOMMY RYAN

Dear Tommy Ryan, this valentine
Brings news not very cheerful;
All in all, it's what we call
A tragic little earful.
I've passed upon your antics—shame!
That night you went berserk,
And now proclaim you've quit the game,
In fact, you're out of work.
Have on hand at least five grand——
Such fines are customary——
With love and kisses, I remain,
Commissioner Christenberry!

From TOMMY RYAN to BOB CHRISTENBERRY

My dearest Chris, it's just like this,
There ain't no use in kickin'.
That referee, it seems to me,
Was due to take a lickin'.
To state my case in this short space
Means problems quite excessive:
If we could meet on some dark street
I might be more expressive!

About the Authors

Xavier Eboli was born Saverio Eboli and was named after his maternal grandfather. His father liked the name Xavier, so that was the name he used. Xavier grew up in Teaneck, New Jersey, and attended All Hallows High School in the Bronx and Fairfield University in Connecticut. Xavier spent three years in the United States Marine Corps and then embarked on a successful business career, starting with his award-winning insurance agency and then a collection agency that remains in business today and is now owned by two of his sons.

Robert Cassidy started his journalism career in 1987, and his writing has appeared in *Newsday*, the *New York Post*, the *Los Angeles Times*, *Timeout New York*, the *Baltimore Sun*, and ESPN.com. In 1999, Cassidy conducted a death-row interview with Philadelphia boxer Anthony Fletcher, who had been sentenced to die by lethal injection after being prosecuted following a drug deal gone bad. Cassidy wrote a series of articles that cited the countless inconsistencies in Fletcher's case. After years of appeals, Fletcher was eventually exonerated and released from prison. For the past fifteen years, Cassidy has led *Newsday*'s multimedia department, earning numerous awards for documentaries on topics such as retired NFL players, the proliferation of MS-13, and mob boss Sonny Franzese. Cassidy also authored or coauthored four books, including *Boxing Legends* and *Muhammad Ali: The Greatest of All Time* (Publications International).

www.ingramcontent.com/pod-product-compliance
Ingram Content Group UK Ltd.
Pitfield, Milton Keynes, MK11 3LW, UK
UKHW031315080125
4011UKWH00022B/50

9 798893 089912